Aloha Wanderwell:

Call to Adventure!

The Nile Baker Estate

Nile Baker Estate & Boyd Production Group, publishers
Email: *AlohaWanderwell@cox.net*
Email: *info@boydproductiongroup.com*

"Call to Adventure" was originally published in 1939 by Raddon Craftsmen, Inc.

2013 Edition edited and compiled by Alan Boyd / Boyd Production Group
Project manager: Betty Collignon / Boyd Production Group
Cover Design: Amanda Mullins
Text Editor: Mark Fletcher
Ebook Coordinator: Tracy Landecker
Project Supervisor for the Nile Baker Estate: Richard Diamond
Special thanks to Carol Ward and Paul Rutan Jr.

ISBN-13: 978-1484118801
ISBN-10:1484118804

Mrs. W. Wanderwell.
First Lady to circle
Globe by Auto.

TO CAPE
HAMMERFEST
NORWAY
SPAIN
ALGERIA
MOROCCO
PALESTINE
SAHARA
DESERT
CAIRO
SUDAN
ARABIA
AFRICA
CAPE TOWN

WANDERWELL-EXPEDITION 1921-1922
CAPE TOWN TO CAIRO AFRICA 1926-28
"From the bottom to the Top" of the World

TRIANGLE
STUDIO-
DETROIT MICH

For additional information on the Aloha Wanderwell Expeditions, including exclusive videos, photos, journal excerpts, and a detailed Expedition Timeline, please visit: *www.alohawanderwell.com*

and 'like' us at: *www.facebook.com/AlohaWanderwell*

TABLE OF CONTENTS

Foreword

by Jesse Bowers

You might not be able to see adventure in the world today, just a century after the last explorers were breaking trails through unknown territories and foreign countries. But that goes to show you how much the ways of the world have changed since a 16-year-old convent schoolgirl answered a newspaper ad for a world tour secretary position.

In 1922, the world beyond your horizon wasn't necessarily the same world you lived in, and the same language wasn't spoken there in many cases. Likely no one had been past your door that had seen the world, shown you photos, told you tales of sheiks, Samurai, cities and tropical islands.

The world was still dangerous. It had diseases for which you couldn't get immunized. There were still forests that weren't parted with roads or train tracks. Most people around the world did not know what people on the other continents looked like, what they ate, or how they lived.

Now you can access the Internet on a cell phone and instantly get all the world's information with a search on Wikipedia, but for a young woman living in a convent almost a century ago, nuns were the only source of information. It's startling to realize that a mind curious for knowledge wasn't going to learn about anything that wasn't in an authorized textbook or Bible.

Aloha escaped a dull existence: She was the first woman to travel around the world by car! Explorations of India, Asia, Japan, and South America had not been well documented yet. You couldn't get information from the National Geographic, Travel or Discovery Channels on how to properly dress for new climates, how to plan a route for refueling, or which rivers and mountain passes were accessible by automobile.

You have learned of the Mars Rover, the cataloging of planets in unreachable galaxies, and seen space walks by civilians. You know that cable TV is full of travel documentaries, and maybe you've enjoyed the BBC Planet Earth and Human Planet movies, perhaps you've learned all about past civilizations.

But Aloha was living in 1922; news took weeks to get from continent to continent, and few people undertook adventures…they weren't conducive to good health! During the next 8 years, she would be part of the Wanderwell Expeditions—camping beside the Sphinx when Tut's tomb was opened, visiting Angkor Wat, sneaking into Mecca, living with natives in Borneo, learning to fly a plane, among many things that few explorers and adventurers would dare. Read on, and enjoy the ride!

Jesse Bowers operates the popular blog "Just A Car Guy" at
Justacarguy.blogspot.com

Aloha Wanderwell: An Introduction

By Alan Boyd

Aloha Wanderwell was born Idris Galcia Hall on October 13, 1906 in Winnipeg, the daughter of British Army reservist Herbert Hall and Margaret Headley Hall. After her father was killed in action at Ypres in June 1917, her mother moved Idris and her younger sister to Europe. As the Great War drew to a close, Idris was enrolled in a convent school in France.

Devastated by the death of her father, young Idris displayed a restless spirit and was constantly at odds with her superiors at the convent school, who tried in vain to transform the 6 foot tall self-described "tomboy" into a proper young lady. Instead, inspired by the fantastic tales she read in her father's beloved collection of boyhood books, Idris dreamed of travel, adventure, and intrigue in far-flung corners of the globe.

In 1922, when she was 16, an advertisement in the Riviera edition of the Paris Herald caught her eye:

"Brains, Beauty & Breeches – World Tour Offer For Lucky Young Woman…. Wanted to join an expedition…Asia, Africa…."

Young Idris could not resist this stirring call to adventure, and she applied for the position as secretary and driver for an ambitious around-the–world expedition led by the self-styled "Captain" Walter Wanderwell, in actuality a Polish national named Valerian Johannes Piecynski. A former seafarer, world class hiker and traveler who had been briefly jailed in the US as a spy during the war. Wanderwell (known to compatriots as "Cap"), had begun the expedition in 1919 as an effort to promote world peace and the League of Nations.

Founding an organization he called the Work Around the World Educational Club (WAWEC), Walter and his then-wife Nell set out on what was billed as an "million dollar wager endurance race." Nell and Walter led competing teams on world tour expeditions, ostensibly to see which team could log the most miles, funding their travels through the sale of souvenir pamphlets, speaking engagements, and screenings of motion picture films they shot and edited on the road.

By 1922, when Idris answered the ad in the Paris Herald, Walter and Nell had long gone their separate ways. Nell's team was still touring in the US, and Walter, winding his way through Europe in a customized Model T Ford, was desperately in need of a new crewmember fluent in French. Upon meeting the eager teenager, he was immediately struck by her charisma and adventurous spirit, welcomed her to the crew, and he christened her with a new stage name: "Aloha Wanderwell."

Aloha quickly became the focal point, the star of the Wanderwell Expedition. Adapting easily to the rigors of life on the road, Aloha found herself filling a dizzying array of job descriptions: actress, photographer, cinematographer, driver, seamstress, laundress, film editor, vaudeville performer, salesperson, interpreter, negotiator, mechanic.... and any other chores that might be assigned by the often tyrannical Captain Wanderwell.

It was a most grueling adventure, carrying the wide-eyed Aloha through 43 countries on four continents. The expedition journeyed through France and its battlefields...swept through Italy just as Mussolini and the Fascisti were consolidating their power... braved food riots and hostile mobs in Germany, a country then reeling from the harsh reparations demanded by the victorious allies of World War I...camped at the foot of the Great Sphinx in Egypt's Valley of the Kings... drove into Palestine, where the Jews were attempting to build a new nation... across the arid lands of India, towing the Model Ts across rivers by water buffalo...Aloha traversed the highlands of Portuguese East Africa, and nearly died of thirst in the Sudanese desert....disguised herself as a man and prayed in Mecca... hunted elephants in Indo-China, became a confidante of Chinese bandits, and was even granted the title of "Honorary Colonel" in the Red Army of Siberia... and hob-nobbed with Mary Pickford and Douglas Fairbanks during a visit to Hollywood.

Along the way Aloha fell in love with Captain Wanderwell – who was not yet divorced from his first wife, Nell; in fact, upon their arrival in the United States, Walter himself was brought in for questioning on charges of "white slavery," which turned out to be a ploy by Nell to force a more favorable divorce settlement. Eventually, Aloha and Walter married in California during the American leg of their expedition. They had two children, Nile and Valri.

By 1929, when they had concluded their initial trek across the globe and released their documentary *With Car & Camera Round the World*, the Wanderwells had become internationally acclaimed explorers. Their initial expedition was followed by an even more extraordinary adventure deep in the Mata Grosso region of the Amazon basin, when their plane went down in the uncharted jungle and Aloha had to remain behind with an indigenous tribe while Walter slowly made his way back to civilization to secure replacement parts, a trek that took several months. The ever-resourceful Aloha charmed the natives, continued filming, and carefully documented their lives. *Her film, Flight to the Sone Age Bororos*, was the earliest filmed record of the Bororo tribe and stands today as an important anthropological resource within the Smithsonian Institute's Human Studies Archive.

After returning to the United States in 1931, the Wanderwells made plans for future expeditions, future films…. but their ambitions were cut short by tragedy and scandal. In December, 1932, the Captain was shot and killed by an unknown assailant on the couple's 110' yacht, "The Carma," in Long Beach, California. Under intense media scrutiny a suspect was tried and acquitted… and Wanderwell's murder remains one of the most famous unsolved crimes on the West Coast.

After the scandal died down, Aloha married Walter Baker in 1933, a former cameraman with WAWEC. As Aloha Baker, working closely with her new husband, she continued her travels and went on to have a long and distinguished career as an explorer, documentary filmmaker, and lecturer - with her notoriety as "Aloha Wanderwell, The World's Most Traveled Girl" a compelling echo from a not-too-distant past when a woman could scarcely dream of a life without borders.

In her later years Aloha carefully tended to her priceless collection of films, photos, journals and artifacts from her travels, and arranged for much of her work to be preserved in various museums and educational institutions throughout the United States.

Aloha passed away in Newport Beach, California, June 4, 1996.

ALOHA
BAKER

THE WORLD'S MOST TRAVELED WOMAN

ASIA · EUROPE · AFRICA · AUSTRALASIA · N. AND S. AMERICA

200 VIA ANTIBES — NEWPORT BEACH, CALIFORNIA

Ravishing Thrills and Dances With Death:

The Mysterious Aloha Wanderwell

By Tracy Landecker

Aloha Wanderwell was an explorer, a vaudevillian and filmmaker, a female Indiana Jones. She was also a wife and mother. She went to places no western man or woman had gone before. Her sensibility was patrician and even Victorian, but her actions were thoroughly modern. Many decades before Madonna, Aloha Wanderwell was concocting the essential elements of "blonde ambition". She was a figure of controversy, self-invention and marketing: The romance that informs her legend is both real and contrived.

Aloha wrote *Call to Adventure* in 1939 at the age of thirty-three, a compendium of her groundbreaking forays into the unknown that sealed her status as the "Amelia Earhart of the automobile." However by this time she had also been christened the "Rhinestone Widow" by the press, as her business partner and husband Walter Wanderwell was mysteriously shot and killed aboard their boat harbored in Long Beach in 1932. Aloha's detached reaction to his death, as well as her subsequent marriage to cameraman Walter Baker (eight years her junior), were found suspect and a bit malevolent by media observers, and a pall hung around her carefully crafted image. *Call to Adventure,* as well as a radio show, were amongst Aloha's efforts to rebrand herself. Aloha was emblematic of the 1920s, the decade she hit the world stage, but she was also a complete anomaly, making her story all the more fascinating and inscrutable.

Aloha came of age in the wake of WWI, the bloodiest war the earth had seen. Nine million people were killed. Trench warfare took military technology to new heights; tanks, poison gas, and machine guns forged unheard-of death tolls. Countless families lost fathers and sons. Survivors of the war returned to their families physically and psychologically brutalized. Europe and America were enveloped in a post-traumatic malaise that challenged assumptions about faith, the future, and daily life that shook a generation to its core.

This deep collective despair found its relief in the expansiveness and almost over-the-top optimism of the twenties. The United States, Canada and Europe became cultures populated by what Joseph Campbell called "fatherless heroes": men and women who, without the love and safety of a paternal figure, re-imagined themselves as "citizens of the world". Not unlike the genesis of the super hero, an entire generation was robbed of its traditional familial roots, engendering a sensibility of deep ennui and loss, but also limitless possibility and a drive to break old paradigms. This new generation was going to make sure the worst would never happen again—the twenties would be their revenge and redemption.

Smashing of limitations could be seen in the huge strides made in technology and infrastructure. Electricity became commonplace in American homes. Skyscrapers began to loom upon the American skyline. Politics took on a globalist tinge. Madison Avenue and commercial marketing, brought to you by way of radio, urged the consumer to live the dream. The availability of credit, and the "buy now pay later" philosophy touted on the airwaves gave way to a sense of power and instant gratification that was to become a distinct part of the American character.

It was also the Decade of the Car. The horse and buggy were made obsolete by paved roads and the Model T Ford, the first vehicle common folk could afford. Adventure and leisure were not just possessions of the elite; now even the middle class could get a piece of the action.

As the war brought seismic shifts in the traditional family structure and assumptions on how life "should be", it also brought women into a more central cultural role as actor rather than observer. After much struggle, the Women's Suffrage movement got women the right to vote. Technological advances like the dishwasher and the washing machine helped the homemaker multi-task in unheard of ways. She was no longer just a spouse, she could now be a "super wife".

At the center of the culture war was the ubiquitous flapper. With bobbed hair and heavy make up, she was a product of the new transatlantic sensibility that had taken hold. She was sexually liberated, licensed to drive, and she smoked in public as an act of flagrant rebellion. Marketing was already placing its stamp on youth culture. Cigarettes, once associated with prostitutes, became "torches of freedom" in the hands of public relations mastermind Edward Bernays. Jazz, a new form that brought a monolithic vitality to music and art through improvisation and the mixing of black and European musical traditions, was the flapper's music.

The arts were galvanized by writers like Colette, who spoke frankly about female experience and sexuality in ways that would be previously considered scandalous and perhaps criminal. Her breakthrough 1920 book, *Cheri*, tells the story of a romantic relationship between a middle-aged courtesan and her young male muse, Cheri, whom she pampers and dresses in silk pajamas and her pearls. It is no coincidence that Aloha, who could have been a creation of Colette herself, quotes the author in the first paragraph of her second book *The Driving Passion*: "Though the ever-vigilant attachment remained, the child savoured life with an independence much greater than that allowable most French children...."

Aloha was born Idris Galcia Hall on October 13, 1906 in Canada, the daughter of a British Army Reservist. In *Call to Adventure*, Aloha depicts a laughter- and love-filled childhood set in a log-compound that inhabited forty acres of lush Vancouver wilderness at the water's edge. The Halls' lifestyle was decidedly unorthodox: They had a chauffeur and a cook, and their own yacht, but the family also swam together in shallows, climbed trees, and lived off the fat of the land. As Aloha tells it, their life was a wilderness vacation for wealthy folk.

Aloha herself seems a perfect hybrid of her parents. She describes her mother as a "matriarchal Victorian seeking new creative life-style for women", which could have been a description of Aloha herself. Her father's credo was, "England expects every man to do his duty...keep a stiff upper lip." In *Call to Adventure*, her observations are often breathlessly descriptive, but not at all emotional. She retains a can-do attitude and candid detachment throughout that comes from life experience beyond her years and an admiration for hard work and sticktoitiveness. She expresses her sexual curiosity and appetite in a thoroughly modern manner, but she frowns upon drinking, smoking or anything remotely "vulgar".

Idris was brought into the cruelties of reality in 1917 when her father was killed in action in Ypres. This trauma helped to mold the woman and the mover and shaker she was to become. Already a tomboy, the death of her father gave rise to her urgent need to become the man of the family. Someone had to be the familial protector, and money and career became a prime concern. Like others of her generation, almost unwittingly, Aloha was thinking in novel and inventive ways about how to live her life. And unlike most other girls, she had the drive, stamina, and stature to live that life.

Her mother enrolled her in a stuffy and restrictive French convent where she became something of a troublemaker amongst the severe and sometimes abusive nuns. She insisted on certain liberties like having her own room with an open window to allow the breeze in. She was outspoken and would defend the underdog in class situations, even to her own detriment.

Aloha found solace and connection with her father in his boyhood books like *The Three Midshipmen*, which were filled with tales of swashbuckling high adventure. She also read romantic paperback novels that told tales of equally nervy heroines. The imprisonment in the convent, the dreary and foreboding post-war landscape, and the unrealized wanderlust in her now sick mother seemed to supercharge her restlessness. Like many young people of the 1920s, she felt a sense of her own limitlessness, and an ill-defined entrepreneurial impulse that craved expression: "What those heroines did! What narrow escapes they had, and how I longed to become one of them! I had a certain facility for doing things; languages were mine without great effort. I was at home in French as in my native tongue. Spanish, German, and even a working knowledge of Italian were acquired with no hard study. I could ride, swim, dance. "

Aloha was also inordinately tall, making her something of an alien. She grew to be six feet in stature, when the median height for women at the time was 5'2". The difficulty in finding clothes, shoes, and a feeling of physical normalcy amongst her peers must have been extremely daunting. With her rare movie star visage, blonde hair and robust stature, she had to have been a target, even on a subconscious level, by those around her—a veritable freak. Aloha never mentions any such phenomenon, and never makes any issue of it in the book. Her height may have aided a feeling of deep difference or insecurity that could have spurred her to achieve more than the women around her. It certainly enabled her to be the absolutely formidable presence she was in situations on the road that would have toppled most women.

As in many tales for young people, Aloha's pivotal moment occurred at the age of sixteen. *The Paris Herald* contained a want ad: "Brains, Beauty & Breeches—World Tour Offer For Lucky Young Woman…. Wanted to join an expedition…Asia, Africa…." Fate brought her into the environs of the equally restless Walter Wanderwell, a Polish émigré who had reinvented himself as an Anglo explorer. Polish by birth, but definitely American in his thirst for thrills, influence, and globalism, his passion above all was world peace and the formation of a world armament police. Wanderwell had obviously been deeply shaken by World War I and wanted to make a difference. He needed a female secretary and companion to film and star in his expedition-by-car around the world. This expedition would be both a vehicle for his exploits and his pacifist cause. It would take a rare woman to match the grandeur of this enterprise, and Aloha was that woman.

Like Aloha, Walter Wanderwell was a paradoxical and enigmatic figure. His yearning was vast, perhaps excessive, and his stamina seemingly endless to achieve his goals, but like Aloha, he eschewed the customary partying and carousing of the period. He was a mystic and deeply spiritual. In terms of lifestyle, he was Spartan and ascetic, but not in his predilection for women.

When Aloha's adventures began, there were other female explorers in the public eye, but none had the sheer scope of hands-on achievement, and the downright earthiness that Aloha possessed. Amelia Earhart flew high in the sky and was supported by an advertising team and corporate funding. Aloha was a creature of the celebrated automobile, and she extrapolated wildly on the adventure it offered. With pet monkey Chango in tow, the Wanderwells drove through dust, mud, and rain, and the fate of their journeys often lay in the hands of the people they encountered on the road. They were creatures of the moment, and though they were often feted by noblemen and royalty, they also slept in vermin-ridden huts and fought off starvation and illness. All of this, for Walter, was done in the name of world peace. For Aloha, it was the "ravishing thrill".

There is indeed a David Lean-esque scope to the tales told in *Call to Adventure*, and also a comic-book sense of constant dances with injury or death. Dressed in utilitarian breeches and flying helmet, Aloha makes her first perilous trip en route to meeting Walter in France on a boat where woman are not usually allowed to travel. She fights off rank smells, cold, and rape. Aloha almost dies from a mosquito bite in one sequence and from exhaustion and hunger in another. She regales the reader with a suspenseful and morbid account of funeral rites in Bombay at the Tower of Silence, watching carrion birds fly overhead. In a sequence befitting George Lucas, Aloha enters the inner sanctum of Mecca, going where no woman ever in human history has gone before, and she enters with little trepidation or doubt. She presents a quality that we see over and over in this heroine: She never ever asks permission for anything.

The Wanderwells were DIY. They funded every foot of their travels through Europe, Asia, Africa and South America with shows for the general public, featuring films they had shot of the location and milieu they had encountered before. In *Call to Adventure* we are treated to a vast array of colors and sounds. They managed to capture worlds of human existence never before recorded. Some of these worlds, tragically for us, no longer exist. They do exist however in the 1929 documentary *With Car and Camera Around the World*, which made them internationally acclaimed explorers.

Aloha was not only the blonde star of these films, she also stood behind the camera and called the shots. She held the nitrate film in her hands and acted as editor along with her husband. By necessity, Aloha was once again smashing customary limitations and boundaries for women.

Adored and scrutinized by the press, Aloha became intoxicated early on by the attention and fascination complete strangers held for her. She was an extremely adept and entertaining storyteller, and her legend drew big crowds to their presentations. This admiration became part of her "ravishing thrill", and another source of adrenaline and sensation, which Aloha needed and craved, and enabled for the rest of her life.

Even in motherhood, Aloha could not summon the will to curb her wanderlust. She describes giving birth to both of her babies, honestly expresses her perplexity at motherhood, and unapologetically leaves them in the hands of caretakers to continue her adventures on the road. From the pen of a man this would seem unfortunately customary; from a woman, it is jarring and somewhat controversial.

Her view of other people and other cultures, though completely of her time, are not always pleasant to read. While the 1920s was an era of ideological and technological growth, American exceptionalism and racism were still the order of the day for the majority of white people. In most of her accounts, Aloha retains the haughty distance of a missionary and an imperialist. Never at any time is that wall penetrated, no matter the beauty or the courageous character of the cultures that either welcome her or look on her with perplexity, and sometimes derision.

Something of an exotic at home, Aloha continued to be anomalous in far off climes. Perhaps she liked it that way. Perhaps there was some safety in being a perpetual stranger. She writes about her travels in Egypt: "Peasant women trailed black skirts in the dust, and their chains of barbaric jewelry swung and clinked with each step. I had a queer feeling of kinship, a feeling which comes back to me over and over when I set foot in the strange, out-of-the-way places of the world. "

In the unique blend of legend and biography that is *Call To Adventure*, whether standing amongst the bitterly oppressed Pashar women, or the genteel British transplants in India living a Western life in an Eastern culture, Aloha is always a visitor at arm's lengths with everyone around her. It is this sense that she retains even to the reader, a heroine who flashes brilliantly across the mind's screen, who every thirty seconds achieves some impossible act, but will never really let us close, who will never really let us in.

Call to Adventure!

Exciting and Humorous Adventures in the Distant Corners of the World -

by ALOHA BAKER

ALOHA BAKER

Author - Explorer

Acknowledgements

To all those who accompanied the author on her first and subsequent tours of the little-known parts of the continents of the world, and to J. Walter Baker, photographer.

And dedicated to those who extended hospitality to strangers.

I Looked From an Open Window

ONE SIDE of my character is strictly Victorian and more than slightly religious: I abhor drinking; there has been no room in my life for smoking and carousing, jazz and jitter leave me cold. On the other hand, I have probably led the most unorthodox life of any woman in America—perhaps in any country. And the whole thing is bound up in whether a window should be opened or should remain shut.

When Madame, the principal of the girls' school I attended in Nice, called me into her private office for the fourth time in succession, I knew there was going to be a battle to the death.

I had opened the window in the bedroom and my roommate had closed it. We had repeated this exercise several times. I had been corrected before, and I had opened the window yet again. It was really a lovely mid-winter evening, with just enough tang in the soft air of southern France to make me long for the wide open spaces I could barely remember from a very differently planned childhood.

"You are American, Mademoiselle Aloha, and no doubt you must have your open window!" Madame was sarcastic, but she gave up on the open-window question. I was assigned to a room of my own. No one in the school wanted to be roommate of the mad American girl who desired to sleep with the winds of heaven blowing round her head, and who preferred a canopy of stars and the Mediterranean moon to the handsome but dust-catching and air-repelling draperies of the school furnishings.

Within sight of my seventeenth birthday, I had no idea that the opening of a window was to be indicative of a whole new life pattern. I had no more idea of a design for living than most girls of my age. Perhaps subconsciously I had assumed something of responsibility at an earlier age than most youngsters. We girls who were 'teen age when the first of the acknowledged dictators set a fashion of black shirts, were also, by way of setting up an enforced independence of action, for ourselves. There was a score of us in Madame's school, although I was the only one not native-born French. We had something in common, all twenty of this particular group—each of our fathers lay buried on the battlefields of France. Each of us had one living parent, many of us had guardians, and all of us were getting our educations at a big sacrifice for our mothers, for army officer pensions are small, even when the men are killed in action. The poor health of my mother had brought us first to Nice, and at the time a minute income stretched further on the Riviera.

"You may open your window as widely as you please," said Madame, and I knew the interview was over, while Madame metaphorically washed her hands of all my future migraines which would be put down to my obsession for night air. I went upstairs. From the window of the room into which my trunk and clothing had been moved, I could see the blue of the ocean and I could see even to the bend of the coast road where it flattened before it started a steady rise into the foothills—there was a white sail that caught a gleam of light from the setting sun, and then my eye went beyond that to the horizon.

There began then a glimmering thought of what the open window in a French academy for young ladies was to mean to me.

I had traveled with my parents in America and Canada, but that I did not really remember for myself. I had the nebulous feeling of familiarity with names and places, but it was only because my mother talked of them. Often she told my younger sister Meg and me of those fabulous days "before the war." Midas days they were. There seemed to have been no reckonings of whether to afford this thing or that, no family discussions such as were common now — if I had a second dancing frock or added fencing lessons to my horseback riding, would it be possible to have a ticket for the concert series? Mother wanted us to have every advantage. Conversely, there had grown up in me a great desire to provide for her the things she now lacked, I did not know how to do it.

I was tall and strong physically, my mental attainment was normal, excepting that Madame's concession of an open window and a room to myself now gave me unlimited opportunity to read romantic paper-backed novelettes which an obliging housemaid secretly brought me. What those heroines did! What narrow escapes they had, and how I longed to become one of them! I had a certain facility for doing things; languages were mine without great effort. I was at home in French as in my native tongue. Spanish, German, and even a working knowledge of Italian were acquired with no hard study. I could ride, swim, dance. With the other girls of the school I attended Mass at the appointed times. And I was most unhappy. The confinement and the deadly routine of classes were not compensated for by the part-Saturdays and Sundays spent with my mother and younger sister. I ached for action, but I did not know in which direction to go.

I had already bothered my mother on the subject of my earning money. I wanted a career and I wanted to become the man of the family. Mother was sympathetic, and I am sure she understood the restless longing that symbolized her own thwarted desires for a life of continuous action, frustrated by her lack of physical strength.

And then among the dime magazines of romance and the paper-backed novels which reached me via the house-maid, I found a few sheets of a local Nice newspaper. In it was an advertisement, and in it was also an interview with the man who had inserted the advertisement. He was an American who was adventuring around the world by automobile. He had a crew of people with him all bent on winning a wager. The travelers were to earn their own way around the world; they had started by taking moving pictures of the countries already visited and were showing them in local picture houses, and lecturing on what had been seen. I made up my mind I was going to see those pictures, for the newspaper article closed with information as to the theater in which they were being shown in Nice.

I did not waste a minute. The scholars were due in chapel for evening prayers in a few minutes. I simply would not be there. Never before had I been outside the school boundaries after six in the evening alone, but now I crept down the stairway and opened the outer door — there was not a soul about. The street on which the school was located was poorly lighted, but at the turn there gleamed the lights of the Avenue, and I followed the pavement to the Cinema Palace, with which I was quite familiar, for this was where the Italian ballet master of the school gave groups of us our instruction on certain days of the week.

I had not a coin in my pocket, so I told the theater usher that our dancing class as coming later and might I wait inside the theater? It was permitted. The man did not see me make a cautious way in the crowded darkness to one of the folding seats. Already flashing across the screen were the magnificences of the American national forests. I knew I must have been to some of them with my parents, even though when too young to remember, and somehow they now gave me a sense of homeland.

The pictures moved on to a storm on the high seas, then there was debarkation from a ship at an English port, there were high officials and cheering crowds to greet the American adventurer, and then there was some of the English countryside. That I recognized for I had visited in England with my mother.

Faintly discernible in the dim light cast from the screen I could make out the form of a man in khaki outfit, whose voice, speaking broken French, came from the shadows of the stage. His story was magical to me. Before he had finished I went out by a side exit, for I was afraid of being caught by the usher who had let me inside without paying. I waited at the stage door. There was a crowd there, but I pushed forward, and as the lecturer came out I grasped his hand:

"My felicitations—what a glorious adventure!"

"English?" he queried me.

"No, American," I replied and added, "What would I not give to have your experience!"

"Why not?" said the astonishing man. "I am looking for a secretary, one who can eventually write for the papers and maybe a book later on. If you know of someone suitable, I shall be at the hotel at ten in the morning." He handed me a copy of the Riviera Weekly, which he had held in his hand. "My story is all told in that," he continued, and tapped the paper.

I did not notice when the lecturer turned away to others who waited, for I was searching desperately in my pockets in the hope that I might have a coin after all. There was something hard which had slipped into the lining of my coat. I fished it out and found it was a streetcar token.

That was all I needed. I boarded a street car for my mother's villa at La California, the suburb of Nice in which she had settled. She was in the sitting room as I came in, and without any explanation of my unusual appearance at home on a week day and at such a time of night, I handed her the paper which I still carried. I pointed to the advertisement and the story. The heading read:

"Brains, Beauty and Breeches—World Tour Offer for Lucky Young Woman."

The whole idea had tickled the fancy of the volatile French. The young lady would be required to foreswear skirts and must wear breeches, and she was to promise she would not marry for at least three years. She must prepare herself to rough it in Asia and Africa and wherever else the snub-nosed, torpedo-shaped steel flivvers especially built for the party should travel. The American flag would fly continuously from the masthead of the automobiles.

My mother read on. The young woman must learn to work before and behind a movie camera—and then mother looked up:

"I suppose you want to be a lady secretary in breeches, Aloha," she said, and the smile in her eyes was sad. I knew she was recognizing the similarity in our temperaments. She, too, was a born gypsy; only family tradition, heritage and ill-health had held her back from adventuring.

"But Aloha, the advertisement says a girl with dark hair and dark eyes is preferred, since they photograph better."

"Mother, I could dye my hair! Let me apply for the position—please let me!"

You are only sixteen, my Aloha."

"I know, but I've been from end to end of the Americas before I was six; I've been all over England and Scotland already—I speak French, I speak German, and my Italian is not so awfully bad—"

"But that travel—that was before poor papa—" Mother broke off.

Yes, I knew it was before the war and before death had stepped in to disrupt our family.

"I know," I said, "and all the more reason why I should start now to be the man of the family—I can earn lots of money and send it back to you—I want to, oh, mother, how I want to go!"

What a mixture of child and woman I was then! But mother allowed me to meet the explorer at the appointed hour in the lobby of the Royale Hotel, and it was after his matinee show that I took him out to La California to see my mother. Of all the mob of women and girls who had come for the interview only I remained. Some of them had not waited for his arrival, for he was late for the appointment, and others had not the qualifications he sought. He wanted practical qualifications, certainly, but he also needed eagerness for the enterprise and an overwhelming joy in living. I had had no conscience all morning about missing my school classes, and mother had set things right with Madame about my absence. So my persistence was being rewarded.

"This is no millionaire's pleasure tour, Mrs. Vernon," explained the Captain when the greetings were over at my mother's house. "It started as a million-dollar wager—but I rather think I shall continue just to show such an enterprise can win out. We are to visit as many countries in the world as possible—we're to earn our way. I don't pretend the thing is any more than a gamble, but there will be valuable records and moving-picture film. I left Detroit a few months ago with the specially built and equipped cars; I earned enough for tramp-steamer fare to England, sailing from New Orleans; in England I made enough to come to France, which is thus my third country. I'm getting assistants as I go along. They may stay a short time or the whole period—that is up to them; but I do need someone to pose in the moving pictures and to appear on the stage when they are being shown."

The afternoon waned; we had tea, and at last mother consented to my going, with only a few conditions. I was not to use our family name, and she insisted that by legal procedure the leader of the expedition should become my guardian for purposes of the tour. There was the proviso, too, that if I wanted to end my share of the tour in Europe I could do so.

That mother's heart might nearly break at the parting with me never entered my head. She was wholly unselfish. She wanted me to work out my own destiny, for circumstances had stopped her from living her own life as she would have wished.

And I was wholly selfish. My only redeeming thought was that somewhere along the way I should be making money, and would send it back to my mother, so that she and sister Meg might be proud of me.

"Sixteen-year old school girl to pilot automobile around the world," were the headlines that blazed presently in the local papers of Nice. I kissed the two-inch type of my first press clipping, and we were off.

There was France, there was Spain, and there was Italy with marching black shirts and rattling cans of castor oil, the wearers stopping our progress to enquire our purpose and concluding we were *Fascisti Americani* because of the trim uniforms we wore. There was Germany, with lines of hungry, emaciated persons standing before bakery stores; there were shots fired into crowds, and over everything a terrible, unceasing unrest. It was like traveling along the rim of a spurting volcano.

We came to Poland. In Lemberg I left the expedition. I lost my temper, for Cap had chided me—I thought unfairly—for a quite harmless flirtation with a Polish officer. But Cap took his guardianship seriously; he felt the trust which my mother had put in him. I took the money due me and went to Paris, and no one questioned my arrival. I went to a quiet pension my mother had patronized when we were children. Madame, the proprietress, was delighted at my remembering her establishment. My height and mature appearance acquired since traveling deceived her into forgetting that in years I was still a *petite fille.*

Paris even then, as it does now, soothed my soul. I wandered about the city and continued to harbor resentment against Cap. Then how mundane everything invariably becomes—the francs from my Polish earnings began to diminish alarmingly. As they shrank, so my restlessness increased. I wanted to rejoin the expedition, and knew I had been foolish to give up the chance of such experience. I sent Cap a card, addressing it to Lemberg and hoping it would be forwarded, and at last I had a letter in reply.

Cap had found someone to substitute for me, but she could not fill my place. How charming that was! I hugged the knowledge to myself that I would be welcome when I rejoined.

The expedition was now in Egypt. They had just secured five thousand years of history on some film footage at the King Tut tomb, and they were back in Cairo, where theater bookings were good. The stay there would be of indefinite length; thence they would go to Port Said, and from there take ship to India.

India! My heart sank as I read that. If I were to rejoin the tour at all it must be in Cairo or Port Said, for it would be hopeless for me to attempt to pick up the trail in India. How I regretted my too hasty display of temper at Lemberg! I sent word to Cap that I wanted to rejoin, and then I haunted the Paris American Express Offices for further word.

It finally came. My guardian forgave my defection; besides he needed me. It was a definite part of the show that the girl of the picture action should also be there in person. My substitute was leaving. Cap cabled me to come right away, but he neglected to send transportation money. That was just one of those harebrained things that spotted our travels with excitement.

But I had no qualms. I had eight hundred francs, which was the price of a fourth-class ticket on a certain boat leaving Marseilles, bound for North Africa. I determined that was my boat; I put down my eight hundred francs and set off with a good heart.

The author at the feet of Egypt's enigmatic Sphinx.

From the 1939 edition of "Call To Adventure!"

Instead of a firing squad, the author is given title of honorary colonel in Soviet Siberian Army. *Below:* Firing a trench mortar in North China.

From the 1939 edition of "Call To Adventure!"

On the Khyber Pass. British troops hold its free passage against wild tribesmen of the North.

From the 1939 edition of "Call To Adventure!"

Africa became a nightmare of fording rivers. dominated by a whirring camera.

From the 1939 edition of "Call To Adventure!"

Marseillaise in a Minor Key

It was no comfort to me to know that the trouble I was in was of my own making, and I was certainly up to my neck in it now. But there is one thing about being born to the life adventurous: The more trouble one meets, the more one dares oneself to get out of it. It may be a vice and it may be a virtue, but I have never had any patience with going around obstacles; I've always wanted to jump them. That a little thing like a balky clerk in a Marseilles shipping office should stop me on the way to rejoin our expedition was beyond belief. If I had really been a young man instead of being dressed like one in riding breeches, white shirt, leather jerkin and uniform cap, with my leather flying-helmet slung on my blanket roll and knapsack, the whole story would have been different. As it was, I was a girl who had had her own way about most things; I meant to have it now, so I sized up the hesitating shipping clerk and waited.

Yes, everything was my own fault. Our progress for six months through Europe had been much too slow and civilized for my youthful idea of adventure. That was foolish, but what can you expect from a high-spirited girl who had just been flattered and feted, headlined in newspapers and photographed for the rotogravures in a dozen countries? Besides, I appeared on all the theater stages from which our moving pictures were shown, and Cap, together with the theater managers, played up the angle of "famous young American explorer".

It was all so exciting, and I loved standing on the stage before the audiences who had just seen me in the pictures — the same figure, tall and slight, and with a shock of fair curls streaming from under my helmet — and hearing them whisper, "There she is!" My brown eyes would blink in the sudden switching from dark to light as footlights and spotlight went on, but the applause was always tremendous. I know now, and knew before the end of that world tour that in the first few months I was just a thoroughly spoiled young person. I had even jeopardized one of the promotion angles of the whole expedition — that of being the first young girl to drive a car around the world and into as many different countries of each continent as possible.

But the clerk in the Marseilles booking office who had been attending to some other people now came back to me, and I renewed the attack:

"I tell you I must go — I simply must."

"C'est impossible," said the clerk.

It could not be impossible. I had to rejoin the others in Egypt because Arabia and India were the next objectives, and Cap's cable had been emphatic about a time limit.

"Wait, wait," begged the clerk. "The ticket is in order, your passport is also, but there is something else." He scuttled to the end of the office and through a door marked "Manager".

I followed him. The manager listened to the clerk, glanced up at me, shook his head emphatically and turned back to the documents spread neatly on his desk.

"What's the matter with my ticket?" I asked. "I've paid for my passage; I demand to be taken."

The manager spoke sharply: "A woman cannot travel fourth-class on this ship, certainly not a young woman. I shall refund the money, or you may pay the difference for another class."

He thought I was dismissed, and picked up a letter from the desk.

"Look here," I said, "I haven't the cash to pay the difference. This isn't the first time I've booked steerage; I don't suppose it will be the last." I hissed the words through half-opened lips and hoped I was making an impression of being tough.

The manager looked up. I felt I was making headway.

"Mon Dieu!" I said. "I have a job waiting for me in Egypt. There's no one in France to support me; all the money I have in the world is invested in that ticket and I can't wait for another boat."

"What's the job?"

I took heart and launched into a description of the necessity of my appearances with the traveling outfit, and told him I was secretary to the leader. We had rated headlines in the Marseilles papers when we appeared there. I sighed with relief—the manager remembered. At last my ticket was endorsed and handed back to me. I hardly listened when the manager repeated three times that I traveled at my own risk, that the shipping company took no responsibility; the words did not register. I stepped out jauntily with a clerk detailed to see me to the boat, and had no idea of what I was letting myself in for. I knew, but took no special notice when the clerk told me that two hundred and fifty French Colonial troops were sailing on the same ship, and the ship itself was no first-class liner.

The clerk led me to an opening in the ship's deck not far from the wooden plank over which we had walked from the dock.

"That's your section," he said, "down there," and he left me abruptly. There was no seaman in sight, so, knowing we would not sail until some hours had passed, I started down the steps, which led into blackness. An indescribable odor assailed my twitching nostrils; the stench of strong disinfectant, damp cargo, salt and putrefying essence of bilge water. It was awful.

As my eyes became accustomed to the gloom, a faint glow of light penetrated from a porthole; I could see in the center of the space a cage of stout iron bars, and stacked round outside of this were iron cots, rising three tiers high.

I was quite alone. I pushed on to the far corner of this hold, where I spotted a tier of cots somewhat apart from the others, the topmost one near the glass insets which lightened the gloom. I chose the uppermost cot, unrolled my blanket, laid it over the bunk, used my knapsack as a pillow and lay down. I felt happier — I was on my way. I slept.

I do not know how long I slept, but I was jerked awake by a bugle call. There came the heavy tramp of feet overhead and stentorian voice shouted: "Rompez!" It is the French army command to fall out and repair to quarters. I tensed and waited. Down the companion steps there came the heavy thud of leather-shod feet; I heard the butt of a rifle bang against the wooden sidepiece of the steps. The first soldier cursed the stench and compared the place to a latrine.

Soon all the space between the tiered cots was filled with *poilus*. The lusty-voiced opinions of the accommodations were given an obbligato of bangs from clanking equipment. These were a rough bunch of typical *soldats 2ème* (second-class soldiers) in misfit uniforms of light blue. They were bound for Beirut after furlough in France. I became increasingly apprehensive as I watched a bottle of absinthe make the rounds, going from one to another of the sweating men, who were unlimbering their packs and loosening garments embarrassingly. I did not know what to do. I was nervous, but my confidence in my own ability to get along kept me from being panicky. I knew I must be seen soon, and now I understood the shipping clerk's excitement and the manager's repudiation of responsibility.

One sullen-looking soldier threw his pack on a bunk opposite mine. I sensed he had discovered me. I sprang from my bunk to the aisle below. The *poilus* near saw the unfamiliar khaki uniform and one of them snatched off my flying helmet with which I had shielded my hair when lying down. My curls fell round my face. A shout went up, and the men crowded round me. I gripped my hands together until my nails dug into the flesh and then a *sous officier* (sergeant) pushed his way through the jostling, leering men. He ordered them to fall back to their bunks.

I shall always remember that sergeant with gratitude. He treated me with respect as he opened a way for me to the deck. To my horror, I saw we were still tied up to the Marseilles dock. The sergeant bade me remain by a coil of rope, then he disappeared, and with relief I saw a sailor cast off the last rope that held the ship to land. We moved slowly; at least it would be difficult for them to disembark me at this juncture. I waited and the passage of oily water widened between me and the shore.

The sergeant, who had made enquiries from the ship's officers, returned. He was bewildered. The Captain informed him I had been warned; I had insisted on retaining the fourth-class ticket, my visas were in order, and he could do nothing about it, and if he could he would not. When I saw our skipper later, I felt I was safer with the two hundred and fifty legionnaires than if I had traveled in custody of that captain.

Now my spirits lifted; I drew deep breaths of fresh sea air, stood up and stretched my arms to the horizon.

"I am not afraid," I said to the sergeant, but I stayed on deck until I smelled stew, and hunger drove me down again.

The barrel center of the steerage had become a mess hall; on bare board tables stood stacks of enamel bowls and soldiers with sleeves rolled up and armed with huge ladles stood before containers of food.

"Soupe!" they yelled.

Sex, thank heaven, was forgotten in the mêlée to satisfy hunger, and I took advantage of food's preeminence over gender and of my position at the foot of the steps so that I headed the line of men. I grabbed a bowl and received a generous ration. The soldier serving me never looked up. I helped myself to slices of sour bread which lay in heaps, and squirmed my way to the cot where my knapsack and blanket lay as I had left them. I had forgotten to bring a spoon, but the beans were thick in a good stew base, so I scooped up the solids with bread crusts and tipped the bowl to drink the last drop. Then I lay down and pulled my blanket up to my neck. I kept my helmet on and did not even untie my bootlaces.

Soon all lights were put out except for a port-side lantern which swung from a hook at the end of my cot. I am an excellent sailor and I felt no sickness; the water lapping against the ship's side soothed me, but I dared not sleep.

"Pst — pst!" hissed a husky voice in my ear. I started. A dirty hand crept over the edge of my cot, and a slip of paper was laid on top. I took it up, raised myself and leaned close to the lantern to read: "Dear one: I love you much. I will meet you tonight."

I watched a dark form creep cautiously across the aisle below me, then swarm up the nearest tier of cots. Indecision gripped me; if I screamed I might suffer further indignities, and I did not know how to call the sergeant. Then fury rose in me, and I determined I could cope with anything that might turn up. The lantern flickered low, there came heavy breathing sounds, and I felt the wind must be rising for the bunks tipped in a broken rhythm. I heard a movement and my heart missed a beat. I pretended to sleep, yet I had my body tense and every muscle taut.

Again coarse fingers gripped the edge of the high bunk, and tightened as the man lifted his weight to the level of my tier. He did not want to disturb the two sleepers beneath me. The face that appeared seemed to have blazing eyes and a wide mouth that split the obscurity of the features. I brought my right leg up and crashed my heavy trench boot with all my strength into the middle of that horrible face.

With a howl of pain the man dropped his hold on the bunk, grasped my boot and we both fell struggling to the aisle between the cots. My self-control broke and I shrieked like a hell-cat.

Bedlam broke loose; unclothed men started up in their bunks, and there came curses, yells, while silently I battered at my assailant as my breath gave out from screaming. I managed to pull my foot free from his grasp, but my strength was really gone when the sergeant hurried to the spot. He drove right and left with his fists, flailing as he came up the line of cots, then he grabbed my attacker by the throat. He kicked and beat the naked fellow unmercifully. Three other soldiers jumped to an order, scrambled into their breeches, and the poor wretch was dragged away to be put into irons. I made a plea for him later, but he remained tied up during the rest of the voyage. The men were essentially decent, when my situation had been made clear to them by the sergeant. They felt the honor of their company had been besmirched by this comrade, so they shared their food with me, and made my cot sacrosanct for the trip by closing it off with a complicated and almost suffocating arrangement of tarpaulins.

Adventure Calling

WITH POCKETS empty and a light heart, I went ashore at Port Said, and in all Port Said I could find no trace of Cap. I enquired at hotels, theaters and shipping offices. Someone was bound to remember if two cars as distinctive in style as those of our expedition had been embarked aboard ship for India. I feared that Cap might have had to go on without me, that I might have missed another message from him sent to Paris.

No one in Port Said shipping circles had seen the cars leave; the American Express office clerks thought the expedition was still in Cairo.

My feet burned in my high leather boots, and my body sweltered in my uniform jerkin under the North African sun. I was hungry; it seemed I always was hungry. I considered wiring Cap in care of the Cairo American Express and taking a chance that he might call in for mail. Meanwhile I needed food and lodging and I lacked even the price of a third-class fare by train to Cairo. I toyed with the idea of sending an S.O.S. to Mother at Nice, but it seemed a shame; I had convinced her six months before that she should consider me as the man of the family who was out to retrieve the family fortunes. I knew even the lessening of my school expenses must make the financial strain lighter, and Moms had enough to bear since my father had been killed in the World War. That tragedy, her poor health, and my sister Meg and I had all contributed to our being in Nice on the lucky day when the chance came for me to join this expedition. I though of Mother now and her unselfishness, covering her natural anxiety, in letting me go. But the plan seemed such a solution of everything for me. Young as I was, I was sure I had the qualifications. I knew how to be a secretary, in a way; I knew I could wear a uniform, and I knew I would not want to get married within three years. I knew, too, that I could rough it in Europe, Asia and Africa or wherever else the specially built, snub-nosed torpedo-shaped flivvers might happen to go. I knew I could learn to work before and behind a movie camera, and I could speak several languages besides English, which was a big advantage.

But here I was wandering aimlessly round Port Said and wondering how best to reach Cairo, the expedition crew and Cap. Of course it was quite simple in the end. I went to the Consulate and showed my papers, told my story, and the young vice-consul with fatherly benevolence gave me the price of a first-class passage on the Cairo train.

I went to Cairo third-class, under protest from train officials. Only natives travel third-class. I knew that, but I had no mind to go hungry, and the difference in the money meant eating.

At last, Cairo. I was thrilled to be in the land of the Pharaohs, Cleopatra, Joseph and Moses, of veiled women and ancient civilization. The whole thing was a mighty jumble in my mind; I felt in the middle of romance when a mob of brown-skinned urchins followed me from the station along the Chara ab Din, pointed at my breeched legs and cried:

"Baksheesh — Baksheesh!"

I had nothing to give them, for I had already tried several hotels and Cap was registered at none of them. I despaired a little, but at the same time that familiar throb of exultancy was pulsing through my veins. I was excited merely by walking amid this potpourri of humanity. There were tall, dark-skinned Egyptians in red fezzes, proud-looking men, defiant and somber; I recognized Copts pushing through the crowds on donkey-back, and I could pick out the copper-tinted Arabs with their classic features. There were Moslems in turbans, some green turbans among them, on those who had visited Mecca. Peasant women trailed black skirts in the dust, and their chains of barbaric jewelry swung and clinked with each step. I had a queer feeling of kinship, a feeling which comes back to me over and over when I set foot in the strange, out-of-the-way places of the world. I knew that I loved Cairo.

Darkness was falling and I was still wandering along the streets, when I heard the unmistakable note which is as ear-compelling as the call of a sea gull over the sea.

"Allah Akbar," rang from side to side of the city, and I knew it was the muezzin calling the faithful to prayer. I watched the people shake out little prayer mats, kneel and place their foreheads to the ground.

Now I sought the theaters of the city, for I believe Cap might be giving an exhibit of the films; he could not be far away, for the Express Company reported that he called occasionally for mail. The first three theaters drew a blank, but the fourth had contracted with Cap for picture-showing, but not for another week. The manager, who spoke bad French, did not know where Cap stayed.

I was really discouraged when I asked to be directed to a quiet hotel. Before going in to register I turned to take a last look at the procession of nations in the roadway. It was then that a familiar voice came to me, speaking in English:

"Hi there, Aloha!"

It was Cap, with his big, enfolding smile and his hand grasping mine.

"We're in camp at the foot of the pyramids—I did not expect you until tomorrow," Cap explained all in a breath, and then we were in one of the cars, arriving at the edge of the desert where the tents were pitched, and everything was quiet.

I could not bear to sleep. I sat on a sand dune and watched the full moon sail in a sky that was like an upturned goblet of dark, blue glass. There were trillions of stars, and not far away I could see the outline of the Sphinx, smiling and sightless.

Cap strolled by. "I'm taking my last turn round the camp," he said. "I've made a habit of it, because the men's tents are some distance from yours. Let's climb the shoulder of the Sphinx; we can see quite well with the moon as full as it is—I want to tell you that I'm glad you're back."

Cap told me of incidents of their travel since I had left the expedition, of the new members of the crew and how they would not be eligible to travel after Aden. He told of being drenched with rains in Rumania and hurrying through Greece and Turkey, Bulgaria and the other Balkan countries; they had touched Syria and then from Palestine had come into Egypt. I seethed with an agony of regret at what I had missed, and I rededicated myself to the success of the enterprise. I felt uplifted and old as the hills, and I was really horribly young.

"We must make enough money here to carry us on to Aden," explained Cap. "I have already begun to seek permission from the authorities to let us travel on a pilgrim ship to Jidda and join a caravan there so that we can get within sight of the walls of Mecca—I know we cannot go any further, but that will be something. Then from Arabia to India—I have an ambition there, Aloha, that you should be the first girl to drive a car herself from Bombay to Calcutta—I believe it could be done."

"Mecca, Cap"I said, not half hearing the plans about India, "has any but the true Moslem ever been into Mecca?"

But Cap was already thinking of something else and wanting to know how I had traveled to Egypt. He exclaimed with horror at the risk I had taken.

"Aloha what would your mother say?"

"Don't tell her, by letter anyway," I implored, and then as a sudden chill desert breeze blew up I clambered down to the sand.

"Good night, Cap," I called as I disappeared into the tent assigned me. It was as if I had never been away, for I felt so utterly at home and safe.

I found that the only member of the original European crew still with the expedition was Jarocki. He greeted me boisterously as I went over to the spot where, in the early morning coolness, I had seen two Arab lads spreading a canvas and placing food of dates, oranges and eggs for our breakfast.

"Allo, Mademoiselle Aloha, Allo!"

Jarocki, short, thickset and typically Polish, was glad to see me. He beamed.

"No. 2's engine purrs like a kitten," he said, reporting on the car which was mine to drive, and which he had handled while I was away. Jarocki broke off his speech abruptly, for, coming from the small tent which stood next to the one I had occupied overnight, was a tall, fair-haired girl so like myself in appearance that I could not help being started.

"This is Marisha," said Jarocki as the girl approached, and I held out my hand to her in greeting. Cap had told me of her the night before. In appearance she was a splendid substitute for me on the stage, but there the resemblance stopped, for her life story was pitiful. She was a product of the Red Russian revolution, in which she had seen her family slaughtered. She then was passed from hand to hand in the easy marriage and divorce of the early Soviet, until the fourth such experience had driven her to dare escape. Somehow she reached Turkey, and it was in Constantinople that someone had told Cap about her. She was half starved and almost in rags. Her appearance secured her the position, but she did not want to go around the world nor to have adventures.

"Peace and quiet are all I seek," explained Marisha to Cap and myself when she told us she was to remain behind in Cairo. She was going into the harem of a wealthy young Egyptian Moslem as his third wife, and she was taking his religion. The handsome young man had seen her first in my role in the stage work at a Cairo theater; he paid her court. It was all quite in order, and many times since then I have visited Marisha in her curious cloistered life. She is contentedly happy, with that peace and quiet which she so desired.

But the call of the open road was mine. Very quickly I fell into the expedition routine, and took over the adjutant work which had been part of my duties before.

"Cap," I asked one day near the 3end of our stay in Cairo, "will you show me the city?"

All these days I had been feeling the intense call of the strange place. There were the Yashmaed women, the hawk-eyed Arabs in flowing burnous, the fantastic blending of colors in fez and turban, the clash of religions, creeds, races — touching but never mixing. I walked with Cap along Chara ab Din and I glanced fearfully down the dark arched alleys.

"We'd better turn back," said Cap suddenly, but my eyes had been everywhere and I had grasped the significance of the sign ahead of us as quickly as had Cap. "Out of bounds for British soldiers," the words were.

"Of course — Cairo's red-light district.

"Cap — Cap, I want to see the best and worst of Cairo," I protested.

It was a shrouded, narrow and garish lane that we entered, and there all of raucous Cairo strutted; the meager width of the place was filled to overflowing. An Arab in a long white robe sauntered along and blew on a small reed pipe which made a sing-song buzz. From open doorways came shrill voices of singing girls; there was high laughter, the reek of perfumes reached our nostrils, of spices and a warm, cloying air.

Cap flatly refused to let me look inside any of the latticed windows.

"I'm a fool to humor you this much," he said, and added, "I only take you along because I know you'd try to come alone if I did not!" Cap certainly understood young people who have romantic imaginations—he let those of us traveling with him at varying times see all we wanted to see, within reason, and then there was no mystery, so everyone was satisfied.

Along the Cairo alley, framed in dark archways, were groups of scantily clad girls who talked and giggled. Many were really beautiful as the dim lights of lanterns caught their features. All were painted of face and some had their bodies tattooed; once in a while a girl, overcome by excess of spirits or a desire to stimulate lagging trade, dashed out into the roadway and danced flauntingly. Cap went ahead at one point to open passage-way where the crowd was dense, and I got some steps behind him because of the congestion of people. Suddenly I felt my progress checked for a slim, brown hand had reached out from a doorway and was clutching my arm in a wiry vise. I could feel curious, black eyes glinting at me.

"Je suis une femme!" I exclaimed in French, hoping that I had been stopped by mistake. But the woman continued to hold me, and then brought up her other hand to feel my body.

"Cap!" I shouted. "Oh, Cap!"

Fortunately Cap heard me above the din of other voices, and came pushing his way back to catch my other arm.

"Take off my helmet, Cap," I said; "that should convince them I'm a girl," for now I was wedged in with a group of half-clad women chattering like excited monkeys.

My curls tumbled down in all directions, just as I meant it to happen.

"Femme en pantaloon!" said the old woman who held me, speaking very good French. She had recognized me as a girl, and dropped my arm to put her fingers on my hair. I took the chance of freedom, and pushed roughly with Cap through the crowd. The chattering girls gave way in surprise at the sudden movement.

"Whew!" said Cap. "I shouldn't have liked to fight that pack of harridans for you."

"The old woman meant no harm," I said. "Just seeing a white woman in breeches puzzled her," but I spoke out of bravado, for I was really frightened; it would not have been the first time a white girl disappeared into those purlieus of humanity and did not return.

The sides of the street we were on converged now and we found our progress stopped by a crescent-shaped archway where there was a native drinking house. Here was music and a girl was dancing. I saw an instrument shaped like a lyre in the hands of one of the squatting musicians; another played a tambourine. Others held reed pipes to their lips, and I recognized the minor wailing of the tabla, which I had heard before, and there were the staccato shrill notes of a flute. The reiteration of these shrill notes disturbed me. I felt exhilarated so that I stepped out buoyantly, and neither Cap nor I spoke until the hush of empty streets brought realization to us that somewhere we had taken a wrong turn and were lost in a labyrinth of dark arched alleys and unknown lanes.

A dark figure slipped stealthily before us, and disappeared like a wraith when Cap shouted to attract attention, for he wanted to enquire which turn to take. Terror, mingled with delight, chased thrills up and down my spine, and then as quickly as we had realized we were lost, we came out on the wide Chara ab Din, found the car and were on the way to camp.

I slept soundly, knowing that on the morrow we would stow the last of our dunnage on the cars, strike camp on the desert, and make for Port Suez.

Ten days later the pilgrim ship Burulos was sailing for Jidda, and already we held the special passenger permits, already we had the instructions about joining the caravan which would bring us within sight of the walls of Mecca—

but no further. That "no further" was so emphatic it bothered me.

Inside Mecca

NO MATTER where I have traveled I have found God. Since the day when the opened window of my school room showed me unknown vistas, the evil and the good of nations have crossed my path.

Whether in the great cathedrals of Christianity, where one is awed by the beauty of architecture, or in the dirtiest kraal of East African jungle, it is borne in on me that every human creature has in his soul a conception of one Great Being. Some see this Being expressed in sticks and stones and the hanky-panky tricks of a medicine man; some worship in secret places, and some indulge in obscene horrors. All seek to propitiate a Higher Power, or ask for aid in following the small arc they know of the gigantic circle of eternity.

I never realized the enormity of the thing I had done until I walked in among the tents outside Mecca and found our camp in an uproar. Cap was livid with anger and his voice shook as he spoke to me.

"Aloha—where have you been? We've been searching secretly in the crowds for you all day; we did not dare to ask openly for fear we might rouse the fanatics who may be among the pilgrims—have you no sense at all? Do you never think of anyone but yourself? The idea of a girl wandering away among a crowd of Moslem pilgrims like this—it may cost us our lives—it may mean the end of the expedition—" Cap became incoherent.

"But, Cap, let me explain—Cap, please, I've been inside Mecca! Listen, Cap—do please listen!"

"I shall not listen to utter nonsense—how could you have been inside the walls? The authorities give me permission to join a caravan, and don't think it was not a big concession, and we have the privilege of one day within sight of the walls. At that we have to wear ihram even before we are allowed to join the camel caravan, and then we are assigned to another caravan for return to the place where the cars are left, and you—you on whom I depend, you in your selfishness—"Cap's words failed once more, and he became silent with fury. Jarocki put in a timid word:

"She's back, sir, she's safe—you are all right, aren't you, Miss Aloha?"

"Yes, I'm all right." I saw that Cap's tense face relaxed a little. "Listen, Cap," I commenced again, "I'm back and I'm sorry—but I have been inside Mecca—let me tell you. You must believe me, for I've seen awful and marvelous things. I don't really know what it was all about, but please listen, Cap—please do listen!"

"Get into your shuduf," said Cap curtly, and turned away from where we all stood. "The caravan is ready to start back. It is after sunset now, and I shall not break my word given to the authorities—if you have been where you say, you have put us all into greater danger than I thought—let's get going."

I bent my head before the storm, and pulled the red and white ihram round me more closely. Without a word more I climbed into the litter on the kneeling camel's back which had been provided for me. Cap might rage now, later when we had reached the cars in safety I knew he would listen to me. He would just have to believe me, and I thought back over the long day I had lived so intensely.

It seemed years since our camels stopped at the appointed camping place, and ages since I stuck my head out from the shuduf and saw the moon was high, while in its brightness far across the desert I could see minarets rearing above white walls. The whole caravan had come to a pause, tents were already going up, and my camel boy helped me down to the hard sand. I saw Cap, Jarocki and the others of our present half-dozen crew milling round where Ferndale, whom the officials had sent with us from Jidda as a sort of interpreter and guide, was directing the natives who served us.

Ferndale was an Englishman, and I had been amused at him. All the short time he was with us, wearing a burnous as did we, he also wore a monocle, pulling his face out of contour as he adjusted and readjusted the piece of glass into his left eye socket. At the start he had described to us in precise words that we would travel a total of seventy miles, going east of Jidda, that we would pass through a long range of hills and then come into the fertile valley that surrounded Mecca. He paid little individual attention to me, but I knew he did not relish his job, although he seemed satisfied when he looked me over after I wrapped myself in the hand-woven, red-fringed, red and white ihram. I was the only woman with the party, but my hair was secured in a net under the headdress and my feet encased in sandals, and except for features and eyes, which were not clearly to be seen, perhaps no one could have told me apart from any devotee of some stranger nation.

"Your height certainly helps you," said Ferndale, and I felt I had his utmost in praise.

Somewhere beyond our camp I stared off into the moonlight-bathed plain, and thrilled as I heard cries of "Allah — Allah!" There seemed to be continuous movement, with new camel trains arriving. A peculiar tingling excitement was in the atmosphere; it was a feeling that surged through me every time I came upon something new and strange, whether it was a new city, country or continent.

That same excitement comes to me still, but now I recognize it, and curb myself with my experience.

Here in Arabia, while the others were busy preparing to get some rest before dawn, I wandered across the hard-packed sand, utterly lost in amazement that I should be in Arabia at all, and within sight of the birthplace of Mohammed, the supposed home of Ishmael and his tribe as I knew from my school reading. I was to see the same spot later when motor buses deposited pilgrims at the very gates of the holy city; I could not have believed that could ever happen, and that a good highway would be built on the sand where I walked a bit heedlessly at that moment, forgetting the camp. I was lost in the romance of the surroundings and fear never entered my head.

We had covered a third of the seventy miles from Jidda in our cars, traveling over a miserable track. The officials had warned us we could not get far by car, and they had warned us, too, of nomadic tribes of Bedouins who were making a living from banditry. The authorities told us plainly that we were taking a risk in going at all. I knew all that, and yet I walked on, attracted by a mushroom colony of tents that were rearing up ahead of me. It was as if some genie had spoken magic words, and behold! There was practically a city of canvas. Here were part of those seventy thousand pilgrims who made the sacred journey each year. An invisible magnet drew me on. I forgot I had felt tired from the camel ride, for I had had only a short one in Egypt, just for the experience. I forgot Cap, I forgot Ferndale; I just felt something impelling me on to those forbidden city gates.

I thought of the incredible voyage aboard the Burulos, the pilgrim ship, crowded to capacity with the devout. I thought of the heat we had suffered in the Red Sea, and the thick, slow winds that could not carry away the stench of goats coming up from the hold where hundreds of animals were penned, for the pilgrims carried their own livestock for larder supply. I rebelled that we should have endured that journey, sleeping on a cleared space on the upper deck, stepping over prone, white-robed figures to reach our quarters, and then be barred from a nearer approach to Mecca. All those discomforts, seen in retrospect, did not seem worthwhile just to take a look at beaten sand and to ride a camel.

I kept moving forward and came out beyond the tents. I looked back and saw that, although the tents seemed to cover the whole plain, they were spaced in groups at regular intervals, one settlement quite apart from the other. And then quite suddenly, as though they had sprung from nowhere, pilgrims pressed close around me, milling about but also always advancing toward the Mecca gate. It seemed safer to keep going with the crowd, so I pulled the ihram closer over my face and strode on. Something was happening, and I was caught up into the midst of the tumult. I felt myself being lifted from my feet so that I was borne along by the weight of the crowd; then I found my feet on firm ground once more, and I was pushed up against the side of a well-groomed donkey, with dull red trappings on its back.

The moon made it light as day, and as I clutched at a strap of the donkey's harness I looked up at the beast's rider. He was a handsome young Moslem who looked straight down at me. I started, for his eyes were not that dark, liquid brown which I thought characterized all orientals. I found out later that there are, of course, Indian Moslems with steel gray eyes, and some with blue, but I did not know it then, and this man's eyes were pale blue.

He mentioned that it was all right for me to hold on to his animal's harness. I held on thankfully to the woven cloth rope, and then was able to walk and breathe easily. My protector seemed to be a person of consequence. Servants attended him, but he did not speak to me, and even if I had known Arabic, I had sense enough not to speak.

We had come to a square lined with whitewashed houses with latticed balconies. People were dismounting, camel drivers were yelling, and all around there were the noises and confusion of a market place. No one would have guessed, from all that was going on, that it was not yet dawn. There was no appearance of a sacred and solemn pilgrimage; all that sense of glory and urgent exultancy that I had felt in the moonlight when I stretched my arms out toward Mecca, was gone. I felt timid as we became caught in a crowd again, converging into a narrow thoroughfare leading through a high white archway.

The street was packed with people and I fought desperately to keep within a step of my companion, who, still in silence, turned to see that I was following. The servants and the animals were left at the wide turn of the street. We passed alley openings, but the way we followed led straight ahead, and presently it ended at a high wall which was topped with flattened beehive-like domes. A pall of gritty fine black dust seemed to be over everything, while money changers, sellers of shoes and sandals, of prayer mats and rugs, whined and shouted on every side. I was to recall this much later, for everything I had seen here seemed to duplicate itself in other religious centers, all of them seeming to have trading marts within their immediate areas.

Now there was no time to look closely, for we were struggling in a mob of pilgrims going through an entrance into a vast enclosure. In the east the sun had risen full and a pink light seemed to flood this sacred square. Hundreds of worshipers knelt and bowed toward a great black altar. My strange companion touched my arm and I dropped to my knees as he had done. I felt no awe, only a panicky sort of curiosity. I had no desire to repeat one of my own "Hail Mary's" as one did when in a vast sacred shrine of some European country.

I knew this must be the once pagan Kaaba for, coming along in the car during the early part of the journey from Jidda, Ferndale and Cap had discussed the whole story. Ferndale had a great respect for the believers in Mohammed.

Now I stared at the altar, which was draped in black cloth tapestried with a band of what seemed to be Arabic characters. Ferndale was to tell me later that they are woven texts from the Koran. I looked at this House of Allah, the holy of all holy shrines, sheltered from the world through the centuries, first under one ruler and then under another. It was thrilling, and I trembled with excitement as I began to realize where I actually had come. Then terror came, for as I turned at a movement, I saw my benefactor striding through the kneeling multitude, going forward toward the black stone in the big cube which is the special object of worship. I did not understand that he was about to perform the most sacred of the rites, which is to walk seven times round the Kaaba.

I got up and walked as unobtrusively as I could through the milling throng which kept arriving and departing steadily. No one noticed me, and I easily found my way back to where the Moslem's servants had remained. They were eating, and came forward to offer me a place at the community soup bowl. I hesitated, for I was afraid to show my hands, but the food was enticing and I took a chance to fish around in the soup with grimy fingers like the others and to bring up a piece of solid meat. It was good, so I took more and was wiping my hands on my robe as the others did, when the master returned.

It was time for me to be going back to camp, but the Moslem pointed to a range of low hills lying just beyond the city. His gesture was imperative, and there seemed no way to protest. I was thoroughly scared. Servants were bringing up camels and I was helped to mount one; then we rode to a foothill of this mountain range. There seemed to be a thousand pilgrims stumbling along on foot and climbing the rough hill trail.

This was the Sacred Place of the Great Sermon—at least that is what Ferndale afterward thought it must have been— but I had no idea where I was, nor had I a glimmering of the meaning of anything I was experiencing. A white-clad preacher, who seemed like a priest to me, was exhorting the attentive and now silent multitude, which we joined after leaving the camels at the foot of the hill. There was no shelter and the heat from the blazing midday sun was intense. I really felt awful.

In a little while this teacher made a gesture of dismissal, and the crowd turned down the slope to the plain, where it looked as though a cattle fair must be in progress. My protector went ahead, leading the way through grunting, snarling camels until we reached the other side of a sort of half-circle where sheep and goats bleated.

In the center of this place there showed up a devil's bloody punch-bowl. It was a large pool of blood and filth, near which the goats and sheep were being slain in some sacrificial rite. Horrorstricken, I watched while the bearded Moslem to whom I had attached myself, selected and paid for a sheep. Clutching a sharp dagger from his belt, with his own hand he slew the piteous animal, then threw it into the gory melting pot. The blood splashed and spattered over the sides of the rimmed basin, and the rising stench was overpowering. There were those hundreds of goats and sheep cut to ribbons — or so it seemed to me; the giant bowl brimming with blood and entrails, and the air rank with putrefaction. The flies, the splashes of blood on the garments of those around us, and the streaks of blood on their hands and faces made an awful impression. No thrill and no curiosity were left in me, and there was nothing to touch a romantic soul in this orgy.

My stomach turned — I suppose I fainted after being sick, for next I remember being lifted to the camel back again. The light eyes of the Moslem were glinting into mine; then he waved his hand and a servant prodded the animal to rise and led my mount away. It must have been about two miles to our own camp; there I dismounted and steadied myself to walk forward, and then came right into that terrific greeting from Cap.

It was only now as I thought all these things over that it penetrated my consciousness that the Mohammedan with the gray-blue eyes had spoken to me as he sent me on my way—and he had spoken in English. What had he said? It came back to me with a rush: "You got away with it this time—don't ever take such chances again."

That was queer. I thought the night ride back to where the cars were would never come to an end. I wanted to tell all this to Cap. But the sun had risen for an hour before we came to the cars and Cap was still unapproachable. At last, after a short rest and time for food, I spoke to him once more.

"Cap, won't you listen to me? Cap—" I begged.

"Get into the front seat of my car," said Cap snappily, but I sighed with relief. I was going to get a chance to tell the story. Jarocki drove my car.

"Cap," I started in, "white men have been inside Mecca before this."

"Maybe so," Cap growled; "a few Europeans, and they were men, not girls, and I wasn't responsible for them. If we get back to that boat it will be by good luck and not good management—at least on your part."

"Cap—you told me yourself that the British have a treaty with the King of the Hejaz to guarantee the safe passage of pilgrims—"

"All right—shoot!" So Cap listened. And as I talked I confessed something that until now had not really been clear to myself—it was that aboard the Burulos some thought had come to me of the chances of getting inside Mecca. That had been the truth behind my wandering away from the camp; the rest had been coincidence and luck.

"We'd better forget the whole thing," remarked Cap. "I'll ask Ferndale not to report your disappearance when he stays on in Jidda."

I became silent. At least now Cap believed my story, and now that the danger was over, he did not seem any longer cross. I began to feel a bit puffed up at my own daring. Ignorance is certainly a wonderful asset for extreme youth—two years from then and under similar circumstances I should not have dared get out of sight of our tents.

Now I was slouching low in the car and my head drooped; I needed sleep and a lot of it, and Cap drove on to Jidda.

Woman's Weapons

MY SECRET bumptiousness stayed with me during our few days spent in Jidda, and until we had a last meal in company of Ferndale. He crashed down hard when I began to talk of my experience, so that I promptly had a panicky reaction.

"My advice, Miss Aloha, is, do not mention your exploit until you are back in the United States—that was not bravery, it was foolhardiness."

Ferndale deflated me so that I was really thankful when the Burulos weighed anchor and set off from Jidda for Aden. The ship was bearable now, for the pilgrims and their goats were gone. We had the upper deck practically to ourselves, and I lay under the awning shelter with not a care in the world. Our cars were safely aboard; Jarocki, who, with others of the crew, was to leave us at Aden and return by the same ship to Suez, was working on the engine of my car.

"I'll have her carry you across India like a bird," he said to me as he set to work in the blistering heat, and now my imagination was winging its way ahead of me. It was all settled, at least in Cap's mind and mine. I was to be the first of my sex to drive a car from Bombay to Calcutta. There was a highway; everyone to whom we had spoken of the plan was quite sure there was a highway.

As I turned over lazily on the mat I had spread on deck, I could see Cap busily writing. The plan was to send advance publicity of our near arrival for use of the Bombay papers. Cap meant to get me a big build-up; he had been in Bombay before and he knew people. Through half-closed eyes I saw Jarocki drop his work suddenly and go over to speak to Cap, then both men came over toward me.

"Aloha!"

I sat up.

"Where is your little brown brief case?"

"Where I keep it, in the back seat of No. 2 car," I replied promptly. "Why?"

"Because it isn't there; Jarocki's been checking baggage; he's been through everything and says it isn't there."

"Oh, well, what matter?" I said. "There's really nothing of importance in it, only my skirt and a pair of folding slippers."

"You're sure of that?" asked Cap, and his voice sounded really anxious.

"Why?" I asked again.

"Don't you remember you put your passport in that case when I handed it back to you at Jidda, after I'd accounted for all of us to the authorities before we got on board? You said you'd transfer it later—did you?"

I sprang to my feet. "Cap, I did—and I haven't touched it since. If it's lost I've no passport!" For a minute I was scared, and then I added: "But we can wire from Aden; it must have been—no, I know now—I had it when we went to that eating place with Ferndale. I left it there—that's where it is. We can send a message to Ferndale—it will be found all right, I'm sure of it."

"I wish I could be sure," said Cap. "Things are tightening up at Aden, and you may be stopped from landing. We're a bit short of cash, too; you know the Aden bookings are supposed to replenish the exchequer."

I refused to worry openly, but privately I was really exercised over my own carelessness. Suppose I never found my passport! And then the skirt—British officialdom was strict about white women appearing in native cities wearing either riding breeches or shorts. I said nothing to Cap, for I thought I might be able to rig up a skirt of sorts from the ihram I still had with me.

Cap went ashore at Aden, and I knew he had bad news when he returned on the police tug.

"They just won't let you come ashore, Aloha. I've argued from every angle. I got the officials to send Ferndale a message, though, and the Jidda officials too—they'd have a record of you with the others of us."

I was completely stunned. I had never dreamed Cap could not overcome the objections; I had been sure I could wait at Aden until the missing brief case and passport were located.

"Here's all the money I have," said Cap. "You'll have to go back to Suez with Jarocki and the others. There's another tip they've given me: This ship stops at Massaua, and if the passport turns up, a message might catch you there. They tell me there's plenty of shipping in and out of that port—it's a pearling station—so you could come back from there."

Cap was trying to speak cheerfully, but this blow to our enterprise was too much for real cheer.

"Shall I cable your mother, or will you take a chance on things, Aloha?"

"Yes—no—I mean don't cable mother and I'll take a change. There'll be something turning up, you'll see. I've just got to make that cross-tour of India. I cannot give up now."

I stood wretchedly watching the winches turn as our cars were hoisted and then lowered to the lighters. "What'll you do for a movie stand-in, Cap?" I asked, trying to joke, and then I bit my lip, for I was near to tears.

"I don't know, Aloha; that passport should turn up on the next boat in from Jidda."

"Yes, Cap," I said dutifully, but I wondered what would happen if the brief case was not found. What would I do if there was no message at Massaua or when I arrived at Suez, for most certainly I would arrive without funds, since we had to purchase our meals on the Burulos.

"I'll have word at Massaua," shouted Cap as the boat sailed, and Jarocki and I kept waving as long as we could see land.

But at Massaua there was no message for me. The Burulos was docking only for an hour or so at this Italian Eritrean pearling station, but the skipper made no objection to our getting ashore and stretching our legs. No remark was made when I went off with a knapsack on my back. I suppose the accepted madness of Americans abroad was sufficient excuse for anything I might do. Jarocki questioned me though, and I told him my plan. I needed help.

Jarocki and I walked together, peering into the dirty-looking godowns that lined the dock and stood along the waterfront. I saw a white man in the open doorway of one of the sheds and stopped to speak to him. He turned out to be German, so I was all right as far as language went. Certainly the Massaua of that day was mightily different from the Massaua of today, which is the big modern port for Ethiopia.

I joined Jarocki again when he turned and came back toward the shed at which I had stopped.

"Jarocki," I said, "there's no message from Cap, but he might have sent one and anything can happen to it in a place like this. I'm going to desert the ship. That white man I asked told me there's a freight boat outbound for Aden at this port on a schedule, which should bring her in here in the next twelve hours. If I can make them put me aboard her, I can rejoin Cap—they'll just have to let me land at Aden."

Jarocki, poor chap, was terribly worried, but he knew it was useless to protest once I had made up my mind. He promised to tell the needful story should the Captain or others questions where I was after our ship had sailed. He meant to say that I had come aboard before him and must be below.

I walked away quickly, for I had chosen a hiding place in a broken-down shack some distance from the godowns, and round which I could see no bustle of native labor. I saw Jarocki's eyes fill as we parted, and I felt badly too. It was the last time I was ever to see him, and he had been one of the most faithful of friends in the expedition's changing personnel. It was to be a long while before the main staff of our exploring parties remained permanent.

When the Burulos stood well out to sea, I came from my hiding place and walked down the front that served as the main street. I found the white population consisted of three pearl traders, an Italian, the German with whom I had spoken, and an Englishman. A lone white girl made a greater sensation in that outpost then than a fleet of battleships would now. In fact, they were used to a fleet for it seems the Italian naval ships came in periodically for coal, and periodically, too, the sailors were let loose to invade a colony of native women kept about half a mile inshore.

The three men gathered as soon as I appeared, and I naively enquired from the German for safe lodging for overnight. They looked at each other in bewilderment, then the Italian left us to go into the whitewashed shack at the door of which I had paused. I found out he was merely doing his duty according to his lights by sending word to the Italian Colonial governor who was located twenty-four miles away. He may have made the predicament clear, but he certainly added to it when he returned with the governor's instructions.

"If the white girl remains in Massaua overnight, she must post a bond for one thousand lire," was the taciturn message. I laughed.

"I have no lire," I protested at this news. "And I can't swim away; I don't suppose you men will leave me outside to wander at the mercy of lurking natives although I do have a gun." I touched the holster in which was the little revolver Cap always made me carry, although I had never used it.

The three men consulted together, moving a little distance from me. They spoke in Italian, but in such low voices that I could not catch every word. Then the Italian returned.

"I shall post your bond and furnish you lodging for the night," he said.

It was Hobson's choice; I agreed to go with him, for the other two men had disappeared to haunts of their own. I wished the Englishman had been delegated to care for me, for he would have spoken my own language and understood the purpose of such an exploration idea as ours. He did not look, though, as if he had a thousand lire to risk, and no doubt the Italian, since it was his country, could make the loan transaction a matter of bookkeeping. I strode by his side in silence to a house where he provided me with food. He offered me wine and I refused; neither was I happy to see that he was drinking very freely. I asked leave to retire to my quarters.

My host was very gallant; he explained arrangements and bowed low. I was to have a cot on the flat rooftop. There I flung myself down fully clothed, and stared up at the clusters of stars. I have rarely seen anything so beautiful.

I think I was almost asleep, and cosily content that I would be seen through this scrape as through all other upsets; then I started unhappily, for I heard the Italian stumbling up on the roof and then heard him sit down heavily on the cot at the other side of the space. He commenced reciting a burbled tale of woe:

"Three years in this God-forsaken land, and not a white woman within miles. Surely the *signorina* would be kind to such an exile." His voice roughened with emotion and liquor; he got to his feet and wavered toward me.

"Keep back or I'll shoot," I said, using English instead of the French I had spoken before. The man hesitated, and sat down again. I loosened the holster of my automatic and kept my hand on the weapon, but I was really scared to death of the gun. Then I commenced to cry; I just could not help it. I do not know whether it was my tears or the gun, or both, but the chap was really decent although the worse for drink, since he could have disarmed me had he tried. I cried on and my sobs got beyond control. I could not stop.

The Italian flung himself on his own cot. He mumbled curses, called heaven to witness a woman's ingratitude and the futility of a thousand-lire loan. I sat up, wide awake for the rest of the night, and very much on my guard. It seems as if the night would not end, but at last heavenly daylight filtered over the sky, and from my roof perch I saw a ship in harbor which had not been there the night before.

At breakfast, life seemed normal; my host was quite sober and courteous and later he escorted me to the ship and made explanations to the skipper. That ship was to deposit me at Aden. I was really gambling on the arrival of the passport, and gambling, too, that Cap had sent a message and would be expecting me to turn up.

But at Aden there was no Cap in the tub which came alongside. I told my story to one of the officials, who promised he would take a message to Cap. Every one of them knew Cap, for he had haunted the offices trying to pull strings on my behalf.

The official was as good as his word. It was not long before I saw the police tug approaching, and Cap was in it. Over his arm he had a length of some khaki-colored cloth.

"Why didn't you answer my wire?" he asked.

"Did my passport come? I didn't get any wire, I just took a chance—what's this?" I touched the material over his arm. I was incoherent with excitement.

"Yes, they found your brief case. Ferndale was a prince about it, got it to me right away, and I sent you word to Massaua immediately. I can't understand—"

"This?" I said again and touched the khaki cloth.

"Oh, that! You'll laugh. The Governor presents his compliments, and requests that while in Aden you wear a skirt—this is the best I could do. He's right, you know; it's native morale. The skirt in your brief case looked a mess, so I had a tailor make a nice one. Everything's going to be all right, Aloha."

I shared Cap's pleasure that everything was to be all right. I pulled the skirt up over my breeches, and held it in place, for it was inches too wide, and thus equipped I set foot on Britain's Gibraltar of the Red Sea. It appeared a barren coaling dump to me, with the white population living on The Crescent, which looked out on the shark-infested harbor; while the natives lived in The Crater, which is the bowl of an extinct volcano and hotter than hell can possible be.

One European woman was pleasant to me; she lent me light dresses so that I went tennis-playing, tea-drinking and swimming, the last in company with a young army captain, and I did that on the evening the freighter was due on which Cap was shipping the cars to Bombay. It was understood that no woman could travel on an Asiatic freighter, but our finances did not allow fare for a passenger boat for me, so Cap and I were reduced to subterfuge. The swimming was all in line with a scheme, and while I was doing that Cap went to make final arrangements at the steamship offices. I was to find Cap's signal for action at my room later.

The sun had slipped beyond the amber ocean, an afterglow flared across the sky and reflected on the terra-cotta rocks; there was a mauve haze along the shore. A netted bathing beach made swimming safe some distance from where my escort and I walked, but I could not resist the glittering path of this purple sunset, and I struck freely into the cove, my deserted escort protesting loudly from the beach. I floated joyfully on the darkening water, and then, it seemed not ten yards from me, I saw a sharp black fin cleave the water. The young officer saw it at the same instant and dashed into the water, making a great splashing and risking his own life. I launched into a desperate stroke; then I saw the ghastly brute beside me. I got a fleeting glimpse of its white belly and snout as I sprang to a jutting shore rock, my escort panting beside me. That was a bad moment.

Cap's chit was at my lodgings and the instructions were simple to follow. A lighter was taking the cars to be loaded at mid harbor. My equipment and Cap's things were already packed in the cars. I was to go on the lighter and stand by until the SS Hankow hove in sight. I loafed in the shadow of the cars, and when the Hankow put about I was already well hidden under the tarpaulin of my car where space had been left for me in the back, the low seat and foot pits making an ideal hiding place. The two natives on the lighter never seemed to bother about me. A derrick hoisted the cars aboard, and it was not a pleasant sensation swinging inward; it was suffocatingly hot under the tarpaulin.

"All right, Aloha?" Cap's voice reached me when the car had been blocked on deck. I scraped my nails against the tarpaulin and hoped he would hear the sound.

I waited until I thought the Hankow was well out to sea before I came out of hiding and dumbfounded the skipper on my appearance, but he took it in good part. Our tickets had called for two supercargoes and two cars to Bombay, and there was no restriction on what type of supercargo.

I settled down to enjoy the long lazy sail through the Indian Ocean. I was excited about India; from all we heard there were enough weird things to keep us busy filming in Bombay for weeks. Cap had letters from some of the people he used to know there. I thought I might even meet some American girls, so I forgot the hardships of the last few months, and drew deep breaths through my lungs, and there came back to me all that exultant urgency for movement and adventure. This was real living; I was now a full partner in the expedition, and it was going to be wonderful. I had a growing desire to visit new scenes and try new stunts, and my enthusiasm infected my guardian with fresh verve.

I fell to writing long letters to my mother, anticipating the mail which should meet us in Bombay; and I knew I was realizing a secret ambition. This was to be the heroine of one of those romantic novelettes which appeared in English "penny dreadfuls," of which I had read scores, hiding them under my mattress at the young lady's academy in Nice.

The Vultures Feasting

THERE was no need of an astrological chart to let me know that this mad tour was not to be plain sailing. I had not been one hour on land in India before I found myself in trouble. It was minor trouble, true, but only for that quirk of good fortune that attends me as an alter ego, it might have been serious. It was this way.

There had been eight hours of fuss and formality before we got our equipment through the customs at Bombay. Cap was fuming; we had already been inspected by a doctor and questioned by immigration officials who had come aboard with the pilot. Now the newspapermen had found us, for the advance notices had attracted them. This was good luck, for the papers could make or mar our enterprise. I was asked to pose for photographs and to reply to questions in interviews. I loved it, tired as I became, and late in the afternoon as it was when at last we had permission to leave the docks and drive to the hotel Cap knew and favored.

This was really the start of my drive from Bombay to Calcutta, so I took my place behind the wheel of the No. 2 car and the engine purred as old Jarocki had promised it would; but amid all the excitement, somewhere in the maze of the oriental streets I lost Cap. I was bewildered by the crowds, the sacred cows that sprawled in the dust of the roadway, the mass of flaunting humanity that crowded the sidewalks, the practically naked children playing in the gutter, and the Sikhs with turbans that I knew hid their long hair—or so Cap had said when he was telling me stories of the strange places he knew, a pastime for our long hours aboard the leisurely ship. I chuckled when I saw the dapper Hindus who wore tailored coats and elongated diapers, and then I edged round a beige-colored cow with a hump on her back, such as later I learned to call *cebu*.

That was when the accident happened. The sacred beast rose right in front of me; I swerved to avoid it. I was traveling slowly, for one could not do anything else in such traffic, but I banged the nose of my car into a horse-drawn *gharri*, and the driver fell off his perch and into the dusty roadway. I slammed on the brakes and sat terrified.

I was on the wrong side of the street; I learned that from the excited gestures of the crowd that sprang up round the car like toadstools in a night. Neither the horse, the *gharri* nor the driver was hurt. I looked round despairingly for help, but all I saw was a barber plying his trade on the sidewalk, with the client sitting stolidly on the curbstone. I saw a bird that looked like a bright blue crow, cawing and keeping up a hopping dance on a doorstep. The noise and the crowd around me increased the *gharri* driver shouted and shook his fist under my nose.

"What's the matter here?" came a voice, speaking English with a strong German accent. Thank heaven, maybe this man could get me out of the pickle. I told him my trouble.

"Move over," he said, "I'll drive you to the hotel you want. We'll need to go as fast as we can; these people can become ugly at times. What on earth wrong turn can you have taken to get on this street? Never mind, I know who you are—I saw you arrive at the dock, and you were headed right when you left there."

I humbly explained how I had lost Cap in the leading car, and thankfully I let the man drive. He was the Bombay manager of a film supply firm, and he knew all about my trans-India enterprise; besides he was keen on new ideas of the sort.

"I did not get up close at the dock," my rescuer went on. "The papers said a woman was doing the stunt, you're only a girl—it seems a mad undertaking to me—how long are you staying here?"

I answered the last of his breathless comments.

"I don't know, the bookings are not all closed yet—some weeks anyway."

"You'll have to watch for the monsoon," said this loquacious individual, who knew New York and considered he knew the United States well, although he had never moved outside the metropolis except on one occasion when he reached Newark, New Jersey.

"The monsoon?"

"Yes, the rains, you know. If you got caught in those you might be stuck in Central India for months."

That was the first I'd heard of the rains; I was to hear threats of them continuously as our plans advanced. Cap and I listened to them all and went ahead. We wished we could have had a battery radio installed in Cap's car, so that we could pick up weather reports as our drive progressed. If we were to be overtaken by the rains at least we would have warning, and maybe our exploring arrangements were not as mad as they appeared to be.

"What about a crew?" asked Cap shortly after we had settled into the Bombay routine of showing pictures at the movie houses and making new films during the day.

"Must we have a crew for this, Cap?" I asked, for I had been dreading the addition of more strangers. "It would be such a triumph if I could be in the car alone, wouldn't it?" And that was how it was decided; we were to travel without a guide or interpreter in India, and then pick up aides when the need for them became urgent.

We remained over three weeks in Bombay and were made very welcome by the European colony and wealthy Indians; I bought two dresses and had them made by a clever little tailor, and wore my uniform only when I was on duty. People flocked to see our moving pictures, and I was applauded when the lights went up and I stood there in person, just as I had been shown in the filmed events. This was heady work for a seventeen-year-old. More than a year had gone by since the start of the tour, and it seemed more certain than ever that Cap would prove his point. It is possible to work a way around the world in just such a manner as we were doing.

There was one ambition I had to fulfill before we left Bombay. I wanted to visit the Towers of Silence. Of all the native Indians I met in Bombay, the Parsees interested me most—the Jews of India I had heard them called, because of their wealth and business acumen. But I had asked questions about their ancestry, these people who had come from Persia three hundred years before. I learned that there are sixty-five thousand Parsees living in Bombay alone, quite three-fourths of the known followers of Zoroaster. It seemed like fate when we met the secretary of the Parsee organizations. He came up to speak to us after we had given the lecture-film one evening, and Cap took the opportunity to put our desire forward.

"Certainly it is possible to get a permit to visit the Towers of Silence," the secretary said, and offered to see about it for us.

"What a dreadful idea!" said an Englishwoman to whom I spoke delightedly of the project.

"Oh, but we shan't see the actual ritual of burial," I assured her; "there's an attendant to explain why fire, earth and water are sacred to the Parsee, and how it is they must not be polluted by the putrefaction of bodies."

The permit read for a mid-afternoon tour of the Towers. Cap and I climbed Malabar Hill, and Cap protested all the way, but the attendant was waiting, and I shivered with an exquisite dread when I saw a vulture hovering like a black dot far up in the sky above our heads.

"Look here," said Cap, who had seen the bird too, "are you sure you want to go through with this?"

Now we were in the shady park that seems so rich with flowering blossoms. It was a pleasant place until the attendant began to talk, and I followed his faltering English with some difficulty. I learned of the hygienic common sense of using birds of the air as consumers of carrion; I heard that in old English graveyards the grave diggers have been known to die from inhaling gases rising from ancient graves when opened. I learned what I already knew: That my own country of America pays the highest price for funerals of any place in the world, but I could not stop the flow of the guide's speech. Here in the Towers of Silence, he was telling us, the ceremony was simple; the body was disposed of in a couple of hours, and the cost was below two dollars in American money.

"Are you determined to see this through?" asked Cap again, and this time I replied:

"Why, yes—aren't you interested?"

We came to a small temple in which there is a replica of the actual Towers.

"The ceremony is simple," began the singsong voice of the guide. "Twelve hours after death the body is swathed in white wrappings is born here by four white-clad pallbearers. Only men mourners follow, and they go to the mourners' terrace. The body is placed on a white slab and uncovered, then the mourners may take a last look at their dead. Next into the Towers of Silence, which are open at the top, and which have on the inside, a few feet below the edge, a sloping cement floor, divided into grooves slanting to an open pit in the center." I watched the Parsee point with his thin brown-skinned forefinger to the outer ring of grooves in the model:

"This is where the men are placed; this second ring is for the women, the center for children. Here is the place the dog comes in---"

"The what?" I gasped, and looked round for Cap, but he was disappearing into the outside shade of the garden where the flowers grew.

"Coward," I muttered to myself and jutted out my jaw.

"The dog's reactions to the body determine if the person is truly dead. Now the pallbearers retire to the hut, where they bathe and change their garments, and the white robes they have worn are destroyed by acids."

"The mourners?" I prompted my informant, for I wanted to get away from the place just as much as Cap, but stubbornness was making me stay.

"The mourners sit in the garden; they remain until they see the three or four hundred vultures swoop out of the sky, then they offer prayer, wash their hands and in the temple purchase pieces of sandalwood to be given the priest who is the keeper of the Sacred Fire, and as he prays these sandalwood pieces are placed within the flames which never are quenched."

I shuffled from one foot to the other as the attendant explained that not even the holy man who feeds the fire must breathe upon it for fear of contamination. In two hours the vultures have their gruesome task complete, and only a skeleton is left. In two weeks the bones are crumbling into their original lime and phosphorus, to be swept into the pit where rich and poor meet on an everlasting level. As the heavy rains come, this dust is washed through a series of purifying filters, and eventually reaches the sea.

Cap went up with me to the mourners' terrace. Below us and isolated, we could see a smaller tower which is used for the bodies of suicides and murderers; so there are some distinctions after death, but the same vultures remove the carrion.

"We must hasten," said the precise attendant; "we have lingered too long. There are three bodies arriving this evening, and no visitor must be here when they come."

No visitor was going to be, certainly not Cap and myself; we retraced our steps by the flower beds and glimpsed peacocks preening purple-green plumage, the yellow shafts of sun slanting to the quick twilight of the east. I looked up and saw specks of black circling lower and lower against the white of those towers.

"Let's run, Cap," I gasped.

"You asked for it, Missisahib, you asked for it," said Cap, but he was truly sympathetic. He held my arm, and we sought out lights and gayety and the friends who were welcoming us that evening.

"Did you see the Towers?" asked the Englishwoman who had shuddered at my ambition.

"I did," I answered, but I never told her my reactions to the visit. Sometimes those Towers of Silence have risen up to torture me through a sleepless night, and black specks hover.

And Horror Multiplies

BOMBAY brought me another type of living altogether; I should have liked to linger where I had servants, a special ayah, and where all greeted me as "Missi-sahib." But our enterprise was settling down into a routine of continual movement; the moment we had achieved one place we began figuring on the next advance. I felt I had my own iron in the fire now with the Bombay to Calcutta dash. Our avowed aim was to drive to Calcutta, but stops must be made on the way. "Cover the ground and get there first" became a sort of marching song to me, and Cap aided and abetted all the undertakings. Besides, I wanted to see everything; I had no idea that I would ever cover the ground again. Yet, of all the points we touched in India on that first trip, there stand out in my memory most clearly Agra and the Taj Mahal; Peshawar and a little old woman who lived in a cave on the Khyber Pass; the sight of a four-legged man that marked Benares forever in my mind, and the coolness of water dropping on my temples in Calcutta.

I came on this four-legged man suddenly, an ageless something that wandered along a by-street and begged mutely for alms. Cap had delayed to take some posed photographs of children whom he had caught in a moment of play; I turned the corner of the street with that restless wish to see what comes next, and this creature reared to his four-footed height before me. I blew my police whistle which I carried, and which was the signal for Cap to come. He came running with his camera still set. The hands of this creature had short projections like toes instead of fingers, and he padded with them flattened on stout round wooden boards fastened by webbing to the backs of the hands. What passed for feet had fingerlike digits. He was no fakir, demonstrating the power of mind over matter in a converted body. The man wore a roughly made cap shaped like a flying helmet which at one time may have been white.

"What awfulness must be under that cap," said Cap as he snapped the camera shutter, and dug into his pocket for an anna to give him. The creature was not old, maybe no more than a lad of twenty, and he appeared to have plenty of intelligence. I do not think, in any land, I have ever seen so horrible a sight.

We were traveling on the Great Trunk Road, and this photograph was yet a thing of the future. The road had long been out of repair since the building of the railroad, so that I gripped the steering wheel of my car hard and sent it careening over the bumps of the very trail Gitana Buddha himself had traveled. Beyond the limits of Bombay on the first lap of the tour we had passed groups of six or seven camels with scantily clad natives on their swaying backs, and bundles of merchandise on the pack animals. Once a chair, mysteriously closed, came toward us, borne by ten coolies. As we drew alongside, a boy's face under an orange-colored turban, looked out from behind the latticed wooden shutters he had drawn apart.

"We'll drive about half a mile apart," said Cap, as we sampled the type of highway and knew that we must avoid each other's dust, for it rose in clouds, caked our faces, dried our throats and turned my curls into a dun-colored mat under my solar topi, a specially reinforced one which an outfitter in Bombay had presented to me when our enterprise was publicized.

When our cars roared through villages, the drowsing natives sprang out of the way, and I became expert in sudden stops while pariah dogs and scraggly chickens scurried out of my path. It was after going through one of these settlements that I missed Cap. My travel sheet indicated a right turn at a place marked Thana, to a fifteen-mile detour. We were to strike the Great Trunk Road again at Bhivandi. I had led since we stopped for tiffin, and now as I looked back there was no sign of Cap following. I turned, making a dust spout as I did so, and back at the junction of the roads I learned by signs from a native that the other car had gone straight ahead. I wondered how Cap could have missed my tire tracks, for his were now clear as day. I stepped on the gas to put on as much speed as I dared, but it was quite two hours before I overtook him. I came on Cap and the car slewed round broadside across the trail, with a sleepy span of oxen blocking all progress. Cap exhorted the ox to move from the center track; the driver slept on.

"At this rate," said Cap, "the rains will overtake us."

"At this rate," I said, "we'll know there has been no other car to pass us on the road across India, and I shall certainly be the first girl to drive it."

We waited six hours before the team of oxen arrived at a village, and we could make our way past them. On the third day out and those following, the heat became intolerable. The country was barren, with low, undulating rises like some parts of our own prairies; a few lone and shabby palms appeared occasionally, and a few twisted brown shrubs. The natives made us welcome when we stopped for rest and food in small settlements.

We made a film in the historic village of Nazik on the Godavari river, where the banks are lined with Hindu temples, lovely and grotesque, and where hundreds of pilgrims come annually, making a miniature Hindu Mecca. None of the natives paid any attention to us. and at the dak bungalow we were made welcome. They were used to strangers. This was my first chance, outside of my Mecca experience, to see real oriental places of worship, and these were entirely different, except that there were the same sellers of holy water and souvenirs.

During the hours in Nazik, I visited many temples, and for an hour went to lean over the bridge where nude natives bathed in shallow pools, while water buffalo splashed along by the river bank, and on the far rocks of the future side, hundreds of yards of crimson saris were stretched out to dry. Cap and I kept the camera grinding, and I posed until the perspiration dripped into my eyes from under my helmet. Sometimes I felt my sight blur with the heat, and my brain begin to feel numb.

We started our drive again; the road was comparatively easy and I felt lulled by the monotony of the landscape. It was at the end of just such a day that we reached a wide and shallow but swift stream, the worst fording we had met so far. It was near dusk and both our cars were stuck on the sandy beach.

"Oxen again," sighed Cap, and he prepared to trudge back some miles to where we had seen a village. I slept until I was roused by the return of Cap, followed by oxen and a horde of lithe brown men. We walked through the ford behind the cars, then camped on the other bank. The natives refused money, but asked for empty gasoline cans in payment. We had plenty, for we had the car tonneaux full of the precious fuel for which we paid varying sums of forty to sixty cents a gallon.

Still shivering in damp clothing when daylight broke, we pushed on from that river bank. The path was of sand and rock, and then the dust surface came again and the cars ploughed through as I held grimly to the wheel. I became sure the heat would overcome me, for there seemed a torrent of fire pouring down from the sun; the aluminum of the car body grew so hot I could not touch it. The sun's rays drilled through the double canvas top of my car, the heat bored into the nape of my neck, and I felt excruciating pains shoot through my head. I was certain I was about to get sunstroke.

I prayed a dak bungalow would show up soon; I had fallen far behind the half-mile limit from Cap's lead. The head pains had become a steady ache when at last I saw the other car drawn up on a village street. There was a dak bungalow to the side; I heard Cap explaining to a native that he needed a lohar (blacksmith), but I did not wait to ask him what had gone wrong. I staggered inside the inn porch and threw myself on the first couch that I saw, one covered with cool matting.

Later I roused to hear hammering going on, and then I heard an English voice talking with Cap. The owner of the voice turned out to be a young Public Works Department official stationed in the God-forsaken hole. As the drive progressed we had many pleasant visits with P.W.D. officials.

I awoke completely when I heard the young many say: "It's the commutator spring—if you've an old spare spring— now if it only works. Ha, there you are!" Then the sound of the engine throbbing added to the maze of misery that surrounded me.

I suppose I slept again, for I opened my eyes as the bungalow boy coughed apologetically and I saw that he had spread tea for me on a low table, and with it a dish of curry and rice. The sun had gone down and I felt better after the food. Then from somewhere an ayah appeared, and she told me a bath was ready and my blanket roll was prepared.

Days went by, the plains seemingly made of flame and fire, the air burning and choking. What wind there was scorched my face as I drove. I thought of shady vales, deep forest, fountains of swimming at Aden; and then we came to Gwalior.

This was a real oasis. The newspapers had proclaimed our coming, and the old Maharajah, who died some years ago, commanded us to his magnificent palace. We showed the moving pictures before him, and I met his wives— official or unofficial I do not know. One was an elderly lady and the other a very beautiful young girl. The city stood high on a hill overlooking the sand-blown plains over which we had come. We were inside old walls which had made this place at one time an almost impregnable fortress. There was the mixture of modern and ancient here which characterizes all of India. And there was also the characteristic mixture of extreme poverty and great riches.

But I got my greatest entertainment from watching the Maharajah's elephants in their daily frolic and shower, which the animals loved. Each afternoon the ceremonial animals were taken out, their bodies doused with water by the mahouts, and scrubbed with coconut husks. The younger elephants bunted each other, and we begged permission to make pictures. I petted a young elephant that nuzzled my shoulder, so that the big beast seemed to recognize me on following visits to the playground. I did not know that royalty from the palace had been watching us, so when my afternoon siesta was disturbed by Cap sending a messenger up for me to dress and come down, I was surprised at what awaited me. Outside the hotel door was the young elephant that came as a gift for me from the Maharajah.

"He'll be grand to tow the cars," said Cap heartlessly, grinning at my embarrassment, while the twenty-year-old beast waved a lazy trunk looking for a tidbit of food. I got the aid of the British resident, and compromised on taking with me a little monkey in lieu of the elephant. I called the monkey Chango; he traveled in the car beside me, and came on the stage when I appeared with the moving pictures. Often he hopped over the footlights to perch on the back of a seat among the audience, and I always believed Chango recognized the Indian scenes in the films, for he chattered when elephants stalked across the screen. I gave him away in Calcutta, for Chango could not come to Penang with us, which was our hazy objective as the next move after this endurance drive to Calcutta was completed.

We made Agra with a minimum of trouble, and we stayed the maximum of time. I had two dreams about Agra:

to see the Taj Mahal by day, and to see it by moonlight. I have been back at the Taj several times, but the first sight of the marvel of architecture has always remained the most wonderful in memory. There is the vastness of the white marble, the incrustations of multi-colored semiprecious stones, the domes and arches that are enclosed by four minarets of incredible beauty. And there is the perfect setting on the banks of a river from which canals have been cut, while the background is always the peculiar blue of the East Indian sky, whether it be seen by day or night. Before the building lies the sunken garden and the marble lotus ponds with the blossoms floating as though portions of the marble itself had fluttered to the water's top.

Seven hundred miles lay between Bombay and where I stood now; seven hundred miles of almost completely barren and dry land, and even Agra as a city seemed desolate and dusty.

The moon was to be full at nine in the evening, the attendant in the hotel told us the day we arrived and a few minutes before eight I asked Cap to let me drive the car through the tourist bazaar, past the Old Agra fort and along a dusty road that ends in the courtyard which lies outside the Taj gardens. We left the car and walked through that superb red sandstone gateway that breaks the high crenelated wall. Except for turbaned attendants we were alone, for it seemed the season was long over. I looked under the black curve of the archway

I moved slowly along the footpath by the shallow lotus pond, and at each step the picture became more beautiful. With closer approach the building seems to change from high to broad and low; and then as one reached the base, it is once more looming immense overhead. At the domed doorway beyond the marble terrace steps leading to the mausoleum, two more attendants met us, swinging oriental lanterns in their hands.

"Salaam, mem-sahib," and I was bidden to enter the shrine. The light of the swaying lanterns picked out the garlands of flowers which were formed with gems, coraland chrysolite, jade and jasper and onyx. There are passages transcribed from the Koran in bold letters of black marble inlay, and a shroud of marble filigree surrounds the cenotaphs of Shah Jehan and his favorite wife. Duplicate tombs are elaborately carved and rest in the upper hall, while the two actual tombs stand in the chamber below, following the custom of Eastern royalty.

One of the guides spoke as we looked up to the heights above us.

"Now we make echo," he said. The men set down their lanterns and sang a harmonious chord, the rich tones floated to the dome, seemed to mingle there, and then float downward on one note. It was very beautiful. The last whisper of the curious echo was dying when the men took up the lanterns and motioned for Cap and me to follow them down the steps to the small square room where are the real graves of the royal lovers. More attendants came forward here, and laid on our outstretched hands gifts of orange-colored blossoms and a dusting of powdered sandalwood. I walked across the room and stood by the tombs where those who can read the small Arabic lettering engraved on them translate the simple inscription:

"Mumtaz-I-Mahal lies here"; and beneath, "Allah alone is powerful."

The tomb of Shah Jehan stands to the left of his wife's, and is a span higher than that of his beloved, for he was a man and royal; while carved on this tomb is the symbolical pen-box, and on that of his queen the slate, for the pen is active and writes on the slate which is inactive. In the Taj the great Jehan has written the greatest love story of the ages.

"We shall take pictures tomorrow," said Cap, and I came back to reality with a jerk. I climbed over the doorless side of the specially built flivver that had its origin in Detroit, and let Cap drive through the dust to the most modern of hotels. I had no wish to jump back into the mundane sordidness of everyday routine, for I was sunk in romance. Nevertheless, I had to become practical. Calcutta was several hundred miles away and Benares must be reached, but Cap had another idea.

Lady Gunga Din

IT SEEMED the Fakir of Ipi had been up to some mischief again along the Northwest Frontier. Some one of the Agra officials said to Cap, "Why not drive through the Khyber Pass? Something of a triumph for the young lady to be the first woman over it — I mean since it's open to women again." Maybe the official was laughing at us, but Cap took him up, and the official strings began to be pulled, so that presently I found myself bending over a map the size of a tablecloth, which had been marked with our route.

"Lots of time before the rains," said our informant, who had traced the route for us. "Here's Agra where we are now — a good junction point; then up here to Delhi, to Lahore and Rawalpindi — all good stop overs for food and fuel."

The Khyber Pass lies eight hundred miles north from Agra, and to the west if one drew a line up from Bombay. Within four hours we had the new plans perfected. One car was left behind in the Agra agency, the other we packed with extra blanket rolls and more tins of petrol which, it turned out, we could have done without. The hotel keeper promised to look after Chango until our return, and he aided us in many efficient, self-effacing ways. Weather news was favorable; not a sign of monsoon in Ceylon or Burmah where it usually breaks.

There were much better roads in the north of India, even the center section being asphalted, and there were filling stations about every hundred miles, so the going was easy but for traffic of bullock carts and unnumbered herds of goats that could not be hurried. I tooted my horn at them, and the beasts spread across the road in panic at the noise; at last I swerved round them without signaling and hoped for the best. I counted oxcarts in one day's driving and recorded a total of four hundred.

It was raining as we nosed up to the barbed-wire entanglements that surround Peshawar. I shook and shivered in the change of temperature, for it seemed almost like a blizzard after the torrid heat of the plains. We found rooms in a government rest house within the cantonment that is the British military and civil section. A houseboy lit a roaring fire in an open grate in my room and I huddled up to it for warmth. This is where the blanket roll came in, for the rest house supplied no bedding, but the houseboy cooked food and my own ayah served me. The curry and rice was good. I slept, and awoke to a clear sky and a rose-red dawn, with Cap jubilant as I joined him in the public eating room for breakfast.

"We've permits to enter the Pass tomorrow, Aloha. That gives us today to see Peshawar; Colonel T. is sending us over a young Pathan friend of his to act as guide."

Our native guide proved to be an Oxford graduate, fair of skin and blue of eye, who seemed to know the States as well as he did England and his own country.

"We Pathans," he told me, "have feuds just like your hillmen in Kentucky, and most of the feud causes are lost in antiquity."

We were in the wide main thoroughfare of Peshawar with draped awnings sheltering its lining of small, open-fronted shops, where one could see a squatting proprietor in each, eager to bargain.

"I do not mind," said our Pathan friend politely, when I lingered fascinated by carpets and silks from Persia and Turkestan, furs from Tibet, shoes embroidered in gold and scarves of woven silver threads; carved wood pieces from Kashmir and perfumes from Damascus.

"Look," said Cap suddenly, "we're back into Bible days," and I turned to see a veritable Madonna, veiled in blue robes, riding a small gray donkey; walking beside her was a huge man, wild looking and hairy, with a goatskin thrown over one shoulder.

"Where do they all come from?" I asked, and the young Pathan answered:"The border countries: mainly tribesmen, horse dealers, camel drivers, and there are others in from Afghanistan, Bokhara, Tibet and the Caucasus."

The women in the street were closely veiled, the majority covered from head to foot in a white sheetlike garment, with two net-covered peekholes to give some visibility and air.

"Women play a trifling part in the Pathan life," explained our companion; "it's far from the American ideal." The young man bent his head courteously to me, but I'm sure he hoped his fellow citizens would think the long-legged riding-breeched youth with whom he walked was a boy. "A woman is either a man's mother or the mother of his own sons," he went on. "Romance, as you understand it in the States, does not exist. Here, except among the educated and traveled, a rifle has more value than a woman—so there is strictest *purdah* for the majority."

Now we were exploring narrow alleys where two persons could barely walk abreast. A herd of goats blocked one street, and I shrank back from the filthy ragged beggars who crowded round us on the steps of mosques and temples. We went down the street of the Story Tellers, and to the Serai of the Dancing Boys, and I wondered very much what the young man with us thought of an American girl who was free to drive an automobile around the world.

The military commander of the district sent a civil native servant to accompany us through the Pass. I felt excited as I drove by the military barracks; then the cavalry lines came into sight, and beyond that the airport. Cap had the motion-picture camera loaded and ready as we approached the entrance to country that at first seemed to spread flat before us, with a ribbon of road stretching to the foot of mountains that looked like dragons' teeth, so sharp and thick were the peaks as seen in the distance. It was a brown, bleak and treeless range, barring the way to the hinterland of Asia. There was no vegetation but stunted sagebrush.

Fort Jamrud squats like a dry-docked battleship at the 450-foot wide mouth of the Pass on the eastern end, where the only passage is that which is practicable for artillery through the northwest mountain range. Here we signed the register presented to us by a Pathan guard. We put down our names, our ages, home towns, the number of the car and the hour we anticipated returning to the fort. If travelers such as we were do not return before the five-o'clock limit hour in the afternoon, then a search party is sent out; if the travelers never return, there are international complications, and the particulars come in handy for the death notices. I could see this Pass was no place for the timid.

Cap clicked the camera as the armed guard swung up the barrier pole from across the road and I drove in. The fort buildings were on the left. A guard house was on the right, and behind it we could see a group of mountain men depositing long, old-fashioned rifles to be stacked against the wall. Each of the shaggy, tall men was receiving a receipt for his weapon, and the passing on with a mien of pride and dignity. No armed Afridi are allowed to carry their weapons into Peshawar City.

Two miles beyond Fort Jamrud came a cleft in the mountain range which the guide said was the entrance to the actual Khyber Pass. We rounded a hairpin bend, dipped downward, crossed a dry water course, and followed the direction given on a signpost which stood where the roads divided. There was no writing on the sign, but a pictured automobile was on one wing and a camel on the other. It made everything clear as to traffic rules.

In six miles of the thirty-three-mile gorge, we had climbed to a height of two thousand feet, and now I stopped to cool the engine at the edge of a lonely ridge. There came a distant sound of music—it was beautiful and impressive— and we stared over jagged rocks to the gorge bed; soon a single gray line of moving figures appeared, traveling on the old trade route.

"Two hundred camels in that train," said our guide as the chant of the tribesmen rose and fell, and the song, which seemed like the intoning of a Catholic Mass, was punctuated by the thud of pack-camel pads and shrill cries of the drivers.

I posed on a boulder so that Cap could make pictures, and speculated on the rich products of the East which were contained in the pack bundles. Then I teetered to keep my balance as I started at the sound of clanking muskets. I was sure the Afridi had descended upon us, but it was only two men of the Khyber patrol. They were fierce-eyed men, whom I examined from their sandaled feet upward. Their baggy breeches were of khaki-colored cloth, and a shirt of the same color had the tails worn out instead of in; the men's throats were muffled, and topping their heads were the many folds of the British military turban.

"Salaam!" The men of the patrol greeted us. They had orders from Fort Jamrud that the younger soldier should accompany us for the rest of the drive. There was a warning, too, that we should not delay too long, since the authorities would be much happier if we were safely back in Peshawar even before the time limit for the Pass.

Now we were bowling along at a good speed, and I blessed the British sappers and miners for the well-surfaced road; the way was clear and I sped around bends as a glorious mountain panorama opened before us. We went by Ali Masjid, nine miles or so from the entrance, and found the road here only forty feet wide between the towering rocks.

We passed Shagai Fort, where fifty men of the outpost troops were practicing rapid fire on the parade ground. There are a number of small forts along the Pass, and a very rich valley opens up beyond one of them. In among these tan-colored mountains we came on a small adobe village with no human being to be seen about it, but on the further side of the huts I glimpsed smoke coming from a cave mouth. Cap had seen it too; he leaned over and touched my shoulder:

"There's a woman up there, Aloha—if you get up close to her what a picture it would make!"

Our native escort made no protest as we unlimbered the camera and got down from the car. I do not think they realized what our intention was, not even when I started to climb up a narrow path which led to a rocky terrace on which the woman was bending over a pile of wood. She was swathed in black cloth from head to foot.

"Get close, get close!" shouted Cap, who was climbing with the camera on a parallel track to mine. The loose stones rattled from under my feet; it was proving a more difficult climb for me than it had seemed from the roadway below. The woman must have heard a stone roll downward; she jerked upright and screamed like a banshee when she caught sight of me. Her face first showed fright and then rage. The soldier and guide began shouting at us. I looked up straining my neck back as my head came level with the rocky platform to which rough steps were cut. The woman had come forward with menacing steps, a great stick of wood raised above her head ready to strike down on me.

I stopped and produced the best smile I could under the circumstances.

"Salaam—salaam!" I exclaimed, and the woman halted, dropped the wood block at her feet and called back to someone within the cave. I could hear the motor of the movie camera clicking.

"Move—keep on moving—get up alongside of her!" he called.

The woman backed to the cave mouth as I obeyed Cap and followed her. I kept repeating "Salaam," just then the only word of Hindu I could recall of all those I had picked up.

Then a quavering old voice reached me from within the cave and I stooped to go inside. A small fire was burning just beyond the entrance; I crouched down by the flame, holding my hands out as though to warm them, and then by the light of the fire I could make out the form of an aged and gray-bearded patriarch. He half sat, half lay on a heap of rags; his face was nothing more than a dark smudge of wrinkles, and a matted tangle of gray hair hung to his shoulders. The woman, as the old man spoke to her, gave me a half-smile, so I knew all was well. They understood that we meant to do no harm.

Cap was overjoyed with the shots he had achieved, and talked of nothing else until we reached Landi Kotal. Here the outpost is hidden from the road, but we could see the caravan serai where the camel trains rest. We stood on the hill above the serai and watched the shaggy animals, so different from the Egyptian camels. Their jaws moved in a rhythmical circular fashion with the everlasting cud-chewing.

"I'll ask permission at the fort to take photographs," said Cap, and then disappeared along the path that led to the offices.

"Watch out for the ugly beasts," said the officer, and I paid heed to the warning, for some of the camels are so vicious that the drivers must keep them muzzled.

"Look out for the car," warned the guide as I drove rather close to a camel. "There are many cars in northern India bent out of shape by a kick from a passing camel."

The soldier pointed out the hills where the bloody battles of the third Afghan War were fought, and told us of the bones of the dead that even now whitened the ravines. We showed our permits twice more and registered each time as well. And all the time, as the officials warned us over and over of the five o'clock time limit, I thought of the Afridi, who are really a tribe of Pathans or Afghans, the fiercest of all the Northwest warriors except perhaps the Waziri. The Afridi are a powerful and independent people of whom it is thought there are only slightly more than a quarter of a million. They are a restless people, seemingly always planning unexpected depredations on the quiet-living folk who are their neighbors. Each man spends his time cleaning his weapons and watching his women work, until the Fakir of Ipi issues another manifesto, and the tribes come down for yet another of those events that make small and big news headlines: "Another Disturbance on the Northwest Frontier — Khyber Pass Closed Temporarily." All of it, I suppose, a part of the price of peace and empire.

The end of the Pass is at Michini Kandoa, and there stands a frowning mountain to the right, while a picket is always at the left. Two parallel roads run ahead to the north, beyond the iron barrier which carries a sign: "It is absolutely forbidden to cross the frontier into Afghanistan territory without proper permits." And another signpost says, "To Kabul."

I took five minutes of our precious time to stand by the barbed-wire fencing and to stare upward to range upon range of towering mountains beyond which lies Kabul and the Asia hinterland. I listened while the soldier assured me that under no pretext whatsoever is a permit issued to a white woman to travel over that road. I turned away to the waiting car — well, anyway, I had driven through the Khyber Pass.

The Scent of Jasmine

THE stationmaster at Benares dropped dead on the morning we arrived in that city. I watched natives painting a whitewashed line around a house where a dead body lay and wondered what it meant. Then as I stepped from the car I saw a huge black rat, the size of a small cat, running in the gutter. We went to the University of Benares where we were scheduled to show our moving pictures of the tour to date, and to give the lecture with the movies. The University was closed, and the explanation was, "bubonic plague threatening."

No restrictions were put on us when we moved the lecture giving to a native theater. The detour to the Khyber had depleted the exchequer somewhat; it had to be replenished at Benares, before we could make the four hundred twenty-nine miles dash from Benares to Calcutta. The State of Benares is fairly large and populous, and the city of Benares, ancient and mysterious, has an almost two hundred thousand population. It is also wealthy from immense revenues realized from the millions of pilgrims who visit the sacred center. For almost eight hundred years Benares was the center of the Buddhist faith, and then in the fourth century B.C. it reverted to the faith of the Hindus, and thus has remained.

So it was that twice a day for four days I pushed my way through a native mob to reach the stage of the theater in which I made my personal appearances. There was no entrance from the back. After the first day we completely forgot about the white circle round the stationmaster's home, and the reports of plague. Chango, who had been overjoyed when we retrieved him at Agra, perched on the backs of the patrons' seats and chattered when the elephants appeared on the screen.

"Will there be any chance to see Benares?" I asked Cap, for the glimpses of the city we had had were fascinating. It lies three miles along the left bank of the Ganges; as we had driven in we had seen parts of the broad stairs or *ghats* which boarder the river and lead to the temples. Over other buildings we could see towering the twin minarets, almost a hundred and fifty feet high, of the Aurungzebe Mosque; and the Gopal Mandir, the wealthiest of the temples, was pointed out to us and there was the Golden Temple of Siva, or Shiva, which is the holiest of all.

"I used to know a Hindu in Detroit," commenced Cap hesitatingly, and I looked at him in amazement; then I saw he was thinking out some way that we might see Benares thoroughly. "There are only two days left, Aloha—the rains cannot be far off now, and I doubt if that drive to Calcutta from here will be all plain sailing---"

"But the man from Detroit," I hinted, as Cap paused.

"Yes—well, I'm pretty sure it was Benares he came to— now, let me see, they might know at the University—I'll make a few calls."

I was satisfied; Cap would be sure to find some way for us to see things, perhaps more than the average tourist. It seems as though the holy cities of the world and the places of the dead have highlighted the tours I have made in strange countries—maybe it was because I was so young then and felt so alive in every nerve that I noticed those things.

Benares was like a vast public Mecca, but the religious capital of India appeared to have no secrets—everything was wide open to the world. There were pilgrims from everywhere, it seemed, and none paying attention to his fellow or to the spectators on the side lines. Each pilgrim was engrossed in himself and in his own way of saving his soul for eternity.

Thousands of years of history were here, and the stores of events before recorded history, when the first Aryans entered India and brought the religion of fire sacrifice with them. Mohammedans invaded the city, demolished it, and then came back to find that it had risen in splendor again. A thousand temples fell before one armed force; and other conquerors led away fourteen hundred camels laden with looted treasure. Maybe it is true, as some of the natives believe, that Benares was the first land to rise from the universal waters of Creation. The temples of those who worshiped running water because of its fertilizing powers, still stand on the sacred bank of the Ganges river.

In Benares, which may have been the cradle of the human race, I came into closer touch with the religious beliefs which then began to interest me. I had had quite a strict upbringing in my own creed, but young as I was then, I was quick to see that somewhere discrepancies had crept into the teaching. I found that the Hindus were not pagan, as I had thought—heathen we called them. They have statues in their temples and many shrines, but there is a Supreme Being in their belief. They have a Holy Trinity withShiva paramount, and Shiva or Siva is the blue-throated God who swallowed poison to save mankind from perishing. In the great temples to Shiva, he is represented by the symbol of fertility, and at the entrance to the shrines always reclining in effigy of stone, is Shiva's vehicle, the Sacred Bull.

And now Cap has returned to the hotel and brought with him the man from Detroit whom he had unearthed at the University. He was piloting us from point to point of the most picturesque, the most colorful and the dirtiest of the cities we were to visit in the East.

"Untouchables," said our new companion as we went down one street.

"Where?" I asked, and then looked askance as he pointed out a group of musicians with performing animals, chief of which was a most miserable appearing, moth-eaten bear.

"They are thieves," said our friend laconically, "black-mailers, criminals, spies; their women have no morals; they all are eaters of toads, lizards and carrion. They are not allowed into the places of worship, they are the pickpockets who prey on decent folk, and all because they have no caste."

"What an indictment!" exclaimed Cap. "But I thought Ghandi was to settle all the untouchable business."

"By the way, Ghandi's at the railway station—he was to stop over in Benares today. Do you want to see him? We can, I think, if we hurry."

And so, before we saw the temples of Benares, our friend rushed us to the depot to see Ghandi, white-sheeted and witchlike of face. He was with his wife and entourage, who had boarded the third-class compartment of the train before the great man got on himself. He was traveling third class, but the compartment was reserved. Ghandi turned as he entered the coach and made a last spell-binding appeal to the crowd. "Give of your mites to the local fund!" he called, and since nothing of gifts is ever refused for the cause of the Society for service of the Depressed Classes, the crowd contributed and shouted: "Mahatma Ghandi Ki Jai!"

It seemed that Ghandi was on one of his biannual tours to collect funds for his work, and like other political leaders he has a natural ability for raising money. He travels, then stops over in the larger centers and addresses the multitudes that attend the meetings, while neighboring rajahs send in bags of rupees for the cause, and small workers offer a humble anna, or one or two pice. Something may be done for the Untouchables even yet, but the prejudice of caste remains. It is part of the religion, and caste may be broken only by changing native belief for another. It may even be that some of the Untouchables do not want to change.

We returned to our hotel and had afternoon tea. That was a touch of certainty and sanity in a sort of nightmare oriental pageantry. We were seeing too much in too short a time really to assimilate it, but we could not help that. We would just have to think it all through later, and then there were the feet of film that we were getting as a memory aid. We were to visit the temples, and to have a trip to see the pilgrim bathers in the Ganges, and the burning *ghats*.

"I'll get an influential aide," said our friend from Detroit. "I do not want to meet trouble when you film the religious rites."

Our immediate goal was the famous Durga or Monkey Temple, the road to which is bounded by the palaces of Maharajahs, and then the wide thoroughfare gives way to a labyrinth of narrow lanes. We left the car parked safely and went ahead on foot, pushing a way through muslin-clad pilgrims who jostled us as they moved slowly, bearing brass waterpots on their heads, each step spilling a little of the precious Ganges water from the overfull vessels. Sacred cows groveled in the garbage-carpeted gutters, and when they lay down we stepped around them; when they blocked the passage, we waited for the humped beasts to relieve nature, grunt and move on again out of our path. Hordes of beggars and legions of ascetics infested the routes to the temples. They looked as though the earth were suffering from horrible sores. Those men with emaciated bodies were smeared with ashes and filth, and others had their hair knotted in hands and plastered with mud. There were penitents on the street corners where they carried out their self-inflicted tortures. A mere child sat, stark naked, on a bed of steel spikes, and an older man lay on a heap of broken glass while he held one arm straight above his body. The arm must have been held in that position for years, for it was now withered and nauseating to look at. We pushed on through the crowds, following the guide, and we paid no attention to that perpetual monotonous hum which is the Eastern invocation of begging alms.

We had now come to the street of the *chauk*, with shops full of marvelous pieces of Benares brassware. I stopped to look at displays of silks and embroideries also, and then quite suddenly the way seemed barred by a high and undecorated wall, while the houses and bazaars encroached on its buttresses. This was the enclosure of the Monkey Temple.

Now a priest joined our party—there seemed to be any number of them waiting in turn to take sightseers around. At the suggestion of the priest, we purchased large quantities of nuts from a peanut vendor. The sacred monkeys, which are often ugly in mien and always brazen, leaped down from richly sculptured walls and loped across the stone floors to where we stood; then they grunted and squealed and demanded largesse of nuts. One big brute snatched at the bag in my hand and made off with the whole store of nuts. The smell from the vile beasts was fetid and overpowering. I let Cap hand out what was left of the nuts, and devoted myself to looking at the stone carvings. Here all the animals of the earth seemed to be depicted in stone, some in most obscene postures. Early Hindu lessons of evil and good were shown in temple carvings. Then my eye fell on a stone post in the center of the court.

"What is that?" I asked the priest with us who spoke good English.

"A sacrifice post where goats are slaughtered."

There flashed before my mind that awful devil's pool of blood and hair, horns, hoofs and flesh which I had seen outside Mecca, and I suppose I went a bit pale, for the priest went on hastily:

"We Hindus do not eat flesh nor kill any animal, but as you Christians have sects so do we, and therefore there are divisions in our beliefs; some of the people do kill and sacrifice."

We hurried on, for we had to see a temple where pilgrims in multicolored costumes were actually mobbing young priests who offered flowers for sale. The heavy scent of jasmine cloyed the air as it mixed with the smell of burning sandalwood, but it was better than the monkey smell we had just left. A lay attendant shrieked damnation on my tourist soul because I took the jasmine branch he offered and failed to hand out the money at the same moment. I had not meant to take it for nothing; I had no small money, and was appealing to Cap for change.

We hurried through the turmoil of this place, then passed beneath dark archways where we could dimly see sacred images set in shrines about the courtyard which was the outer court of the holy of holies. A few yards from this a strong whiff of a barnyard reached us, and we could see a sleek, young and apparently much overfed sacred cow nuzzling and slobbering as it bumped into newly arrived worshipers who offered the animal sweets and pastry. I wondered if the beast ate hay, like ordinary cows, but I did not dare to ask the guide.

Now we saw silver doors gleaming in the light of oil lamps, and as they opened to the hands of more priests, we found ourselves under a vast golden dome. Immediately in the center of the floor space we saw a single shaft of black marble garlanded with white jasmine wreaths. This is the emblem of the deity to which the temple is dedicated. It was mystical and strange, and became more so as temple bells commenced to ring and there came the chanting of Vedic hymns. One began to forget the filth and confusion in the outer courts. Later at the hotel, I pressed my jasmine spray between the pages of my diary. There was a fragrance about the dead blossoms for a long time.

Idris Galcia Hall, AKA Aloha Wanderwell, 1922

Aloha and "Cap" Walter Wanderwell, 1924

Captain Walter Wanderwell, (AKA Valerian Johannes Piecynski), 1924

Cap with camera, India, 1924

Preparing to cross the Yangtse River, 1924

Cap and Aloha with "Chango."

The Wanderwell International Police expeditions now comprise five Auto Units, two Motocycle Units and one Bycicle Unit with over 100 active members en route on five continents.

From a vintage Wanderwell Expedition souvenir book

Greeting the American World Flyers, Calcutta, 1924

"Joking with Kenya Colony East Africa Kavirondo Chief"

India, 1924

Japan, 1924

Africa, 1927

ALOHA WANDERWELL

first girl to have girdled the globe by auto

1922—1929

**43 COUNTRIES
4 CONTINENTS**

Well, We Made It

IT WAS daybreak. We left the car at the top of stone steps that led to a primitive wooden landing stage. Between native boats was moored a larger craft on which a flat-roofed cabin was covered by a tent-like awning. Our hosts gave sharp orders and the boat came alongside. Our Detroit friend had planned a surprise, and we stayed over one more day in Benares to benefit by it. We were the guests of a Hindu of high position for a tour of the Ganges and the burning *ghats*.

The boat deck was covered with gold-colored matting and there were cushions to be used as seats; there was a lunch basket and a container of cool drinks, and a Primus stove to make the hot tea which everyone drinks during the hottest Indian weather. There were paper fans, fly swatters and cigarettes. To our hosts I was an oddity, for I did not smoke and did not drink wine. They could not understand the anomaly of a girl who was attempting to drive a car around the world, and yet who was Victorian at heart. We cast off from the jetty with eight oarsmen pushing our unwieldy craft slowly into midstream. I hardly glanced at the towering temples and palaces along the banks, and scarcely heard the well-bred softly accented phrases of my host, who explained the historic background to these masses of masonry. I was engrossed in watching the hundreds of half nude natives congregated at the foot of wide steps leading up from the water's edge. They immersed themselves in the dark, sluggish waters; the recital of prayers carried to us across the stream. Some of the men cleansed themselves as though in a bath-tub; others scooped up the filthy-looking liquid in their hands, then quenched their thirst or used the water as a dentifrice, spitting it back to its source. Women in bright saris that clung wetly to their forms bobbed about and splashed, and the silver and gold ornaments on their arms and ankles clashed musically. We tied up where a group of women hurriedly replaced their wet garments with dry saris, and four tiny girls capered in a shallow part, their garment each a string across a fat tummy and from the string a silver pendant hanging. They halted their play and stared solemnly from big brown eyes fringed with long black eyelashes. They refused to smile in response to our greeting.

On the steps of the bathing *ghats* were endless rows of straw umbrellas looking like giant toadstools, while under each squatted a yellow, gnomelike priest dispensing blessings with one hand and gathering in silver coins with the other, stopping at intervals to issue certificates of purification to pilgrims who toiled up the steps from the river, each pilgrim with his shining brass urn of sacred Ganges water. I marveled at the devotion to this great symbol of eternal life to the Hindu.

It was midday now and already the color scheme was changing from the soft brown tints of dawn to yellow and ocher shadows. We could not delay, since our start for Calcutta was to be early the following morning, and we had yet to see the burning *ghats*. I shook the perspiration from my eyes and steeled myself for the making of film scenes where bodies of Hindu dead are placed on pyres of burning wood for cremation.

We rounded a bend in the river and I saw on the bank blue streaks of smoke curling upward slowly. It stood out against the almost deserted background of temples and terraces, and then I watched a few white clad figures move near the smoking piles of wood. Two small boys in the foreground waded waist deep in the greasy, black, ash-strewn water at the river's edge. We saw small shrines erected in memory of the self-immolation of Hindu widows, but suttee is forbidden by the British raj, and no longer do bereaved women throw themselves on a dead husband's pyre.

Cap set the camera and the soft whir of the motor was the only sound. A perfect scene for our purposes unfolded itself, for a funeral procession started down toward the river. The bearers of the body wore white garments, and carried a long pole to which the corpse was strapped, the form swathed in white cloth. The group reached the last step, four men advanced into the river, and slid the muslin shrouded body into the water, the immersion lasting no longer than a minute. Our camera hummed softly as the mourners glared angrily at us as they carried their dripping burden to a pile of unlighted wood. The bearers gathered up their wet dhotis and strode off, while the body lay atop the pile; a lonely stoker hovered near, but there was no fire.

"Probably the dead man's son," whispered our Hindu host, as a young man returned carrying a blazing torch. He thrust this deep at the base of the crisscrossed faggots. He bowed his head, turned and walked back slowly the way he had come, then blackening gobs of smoke rose in heavy puffs. Little flames now were sparkling red and yellow, shooting up among the timbers, twigs on the lighter boughs ignited, tongues of flame leaped from side to side of the pyre and the muslin shroud vanished in an angry crackling blaze. The stoker used his long pole to stir smoldering embers and to keep half-charred faggots in position. We filmed for two hours. The stench was frightful. When we ran out of film, I had seen enough.

"Sometimes," said our host, "when relatives are too poor to buy sufficient wood to have the body completely burned, the charred remains are tied with string by small boy bathers,

then towed by boat out to midstream where they are cast
adrift in the current and are borne out to sea."

I was not sorry to leave Benares, although the plain
beyond the city over which the first part of our road lay, was
a mass of seeming flame and fire, the very air in my nostrils
seemed to burn and choke me, for the wind scorched as it
blew. The car became so hot I could not touch it with my
bare hand, but the motors hummed smoothly in both cars
after their overhauling in the Benares workshops. We were
on the way to Calcutta, the last lap of our journey in India,
and we had to hurry, for the news of the monsoon was not
reassuring. As the miles and days went by, I hung on grimly
to the steering wheel, and wondered how far ahead Cap
might have reached, for I was beginning to see those familiar
visions of shady vales, deep forests and rushing streams.

At our last stop Cap had said: "You take it a bit slower,
Aloha; I'll drive ahead and find a dak bungalow. You need a
good meal." We had been living on roasted soy beans, only
two teaspoonfuls being needed for a full meal. This cut
down on our equipment and saved time; we jettisoned
everything possible, too, from the cars, for the road was bad,
a patchwork of holes and gulleys. We had now covered
twelve hundred miles from Bombay, not counting the detour
to Peshawar and the Khyber Pass, and I began to doubt that
I would be the first girl to drive the cross-India stretch, for
there were two hundred miles to go, and I was weary. We
were racing now with a line of sodden clouds behind us;
they seemed to grow darker and heavier every minute, and
the heat increased. I wondered what would happen if I
screamed with exhaustion; then I set my teeth, for it would
have been shameful to give up after getting so far.

At last we were in Bengal, with lovely jungle glades on
either side of the roadway which at times became no more
than a rutted track. Tinted butterflies almost dazzled the
eyes as they flitted like animated jewels across the shafts of
sunlight that pierced the green shadow. I honked my horn
and there set up a scream from jungle creatures; I caught

sight of monkeys swinging from branches and chattering. I shortened Chango's leash, and he chattered back, then cowered down beside me at some shriek more raucous than the others. We passed familiar-looking lettered boards with gangs of workmen loitering under the eyes of native foremen. "P.W.D.," ran the alphabetical description, and the natives prodding at heaps of stone and gravel purporting to be road-repair work, straightened their backs and lolled against their shovels to watch the extraordinary appearance of a girl at the wheel of a dust-covered car, and a monkey chattering on the seat beside her.

Cap's car had disappeared, and I spurted after him; it was getting close to dusk and there seemed to be mile on mile of more closely overhung jungle. I thought of tigers and pythons, and my head ached from the touch of sun I had had before; my eyes adjusted badly to the dim light. And then my car bounded with terrific force and stopped as the wheel slewed round in my hands. I fell halfway across the seat, but I had sense left to shut off the ignition. Chango squealed and jumped about wildly. Slowly the car, which had been tilted, righted itself, then settled with a little plop back into the dust. I got down stiffly and walked around the boulder, as I thought, against which I had run. The boulder was a water buffalo, a young-looking, thin thing that must have been wallowing in the dust, and now it was dead. I shivered in apprehension that some of the road menders would come into sight. If a buffalo was in the road it meant there must be a village near, and I knew there was a fifty-rupee fine for injury to one of these brutes. I shivered again, for the natives become furious when one of their sacred animals is hurt; the only safety from their wrath lies in flight to the next province.

There was nothing to do but go ahead. I had to overtake Cap. I got into the car, and, thank heaven, the engine turned over. I released the gears and traveled carefully and slowly, leaving the big animal behind. I came to a village and as I passed the police bungalow, an inspiration came to me. I stopped the car, went inside the building and reported a dead buffalo lying on the road over which I had traveled, and the policeman thanked me profusely for the information. I hope that black water buffalo was really dead before my car hit it—but I do not think it was.

Cap was already at the dak bungalow; he reported another hundred and fifty miles to go, and the clouds were gathering in strength. Even as I went into the bungalow for an hour's rest, a few drops of rain fell, and I fancied the dust hissed as the water touched it. When I came out again, the rain was falling in a solid sheet.

"Do you want to give it up, Aloha?" Cap peered at me through a veil of falling water while I wrapped Chango in a piece of tarpaulin, and looked round. In the minutes since the rain had begun to fall, it seemed as if all Nature had changed. I could see the seared trees becoming green before my eyes, and strange-looking lizards and bugs were crawling from under the rocks. I filled my lungs with a long, cooling breath.

"I'm sure I can do it, Cap. I'd hate to give up—anyhow the newspapers have the story now, and I should hate to fail."

"I could leave this car, you know, and drive yours." Cap was hesitant and worried.

"No, that would not be the same thing. You've featured me as the first girl to drive the Bombay-to-Calcutta road alone, and I just have to do it."

For twenty-four hours there was a steady downpour which never slackened; everything was drenched, and the car seemed full of mud. Cap broke the trail, but the roiling liquid dust filled in his wheel tracks as soon as the car had passed. My wheels skidded wildly and slewed round a dozen times, and with infinite labor I would get myself headed south again and go on. Chango kept up a continuous whimpering and shivering.

Cap was waiting in another village. The guidebook promised a river to be crossed soon, but this time a bridge was designated, and we congratulated ourselves there would not be another experience of natives hauling, and toiling water buffalo dragging our cars across a precarious fording place. At the other side of the river the highway was good, so the guidebook stated.

We came to the village on the north side of the river just at dusk, and found the bridge had been carried away by flood the day before. To get across we were offered the use of the railroad trestle. The officials were helpful and assured us the trestle had been crossed by car before. There was one alternative to this—that we wait three days, when flat cars and an engine were expected; the motors could be lifted on the flat cars and the whole outfit taken across. But the radio warned amid crackling static that the rains were to become worse. There was every chance that the railroad trestle bridge might be carried off too. I looked at the high bridge and wondered where I would get the nerve to cross on those ties; then I looked about the village where we would have to stay if we did not go on, and I decided it would need more courage to stay.

The railroad company added us to their schedule, and provided the automobiles with red and green lanterns and a brakeman each. Natives built a ramp for the cars to reach the trestle, and other natives walked across to build yet another ramp on the further side so that we could get off the height.

Beyond the Sone River we plunged into a sea of mud, the wheels thrashed round, and sprays of mud shot up over the fender-less sides of the car and drenched me. Chango was terrified, but I think the little monkey comforted me, for when I encouraged him with words I felt braver myself.

It was now forty-eight hours since the rains had commenced, and we had continued driving night and day, without any halt for sleep. There was never time to get my clothing dried out, and I felt glued to the seat while each limb ached and periodic shivers ran along my spine so that the steering wheel jittered in my grasp. I felt sure someone would have to pry my fingers loose.

We halted in the shelter of a colossal bamboo forest, and Cap walked back to my car:

"Calcutta tonight, Aloha; just sixteen miles more to the outskirts of the city."

Abruptly we came on paved road, with rows of houses on either side, and scores of people scurrying along to seek shelter. The tires were running over smooth asphalt pavement, and the rain sluiced off the mud from the tarpaulins in which I had wrapped myself. This was Calcutta.

I Glimpse the Pearly Gates

I OPENED my eyes and marveled at the still coolness all about me. There was a white ceiling above, and white walls with a few pieces of furniture close against them. I felt an excruciating pain that the base of my skull, and tried to lift my hand to my head but it was too heavy to get it up and my shoulder joints seemed to creak when I attempted to move. I was sore all over. Something screamed and jumped excitedly down at my feet.

Someone put a pleasant liquid to my lips, and a smiling ayah bent over me, speaking softly: "Missi-sahib is better." I could feel myself relaxing into sleep

When next I opened my eyes Chango was beside me, his small brown eyes glinting at me with curiosity and hopefulness. I moved my arm and it did not hurt. As I touched the monkey he shrieked with delight. Then I head a step and there was Cap.

"Feel better, old lady?" He added in a casual tone: "You gave us a fright, thought you were going to slip away on us, but now the doctor says you are okay—you overdid things a bit."

"Where am I?" I asked.

"You're with friends of mine, and Mrs. J. hired the ayah for you. You don't remember anything after you stopped the car, do you?"

"How long have I been here?" I said.

"Three days; you were just exhausted. The newspaper men are clamoring for stores from you—I told them you would be up tomorrow.

Somehow I knew Cap had been worried about me, but now I felt all right and the old energy and sense of expectancy was creeping back.

"Waken me early, ayah," I told the kindly native woman, and it seemed only minutes until it was broad daylight and I was struggling into my boots and breeches, magically free of mud.

The easy, comfortable European style of life in Calcutta enfolded me. Each morning I wakened in my fine straw matting bed under a waving punka, and the ayah served my chota haz'ri (fresh fruit and tea), then in a couple of hours came breakfast on a shady verandah with my hostess; chai at eleven in the morning with friends coming in to gossip and more newspaper men getting information from me and more photographs. Tiffin was at one o'clock, and in the late afternoon I went to afternoon teas in the homes of European women who looked wan and frail, but who plied me with a thousand questions about this rigorous life. They shaded their heads with parasols when the weather was fine enough to go into their lovely gardens, like a bit of transplanted England, and they sipped their tea from cups held in hands encased in long white gloves.

I tried to explain why traveling fascinated me, but I could not find words to express that insatiable desire for new countries, and that intangible sense of kinship which I have for strangers and the strange places of new continents. I told the women of my excitement at the thought of going to Penang and Indo-China, and then to China, Siberia, Japan and perhaps to other countries before we reached the United States. And although America was my birthplace, that was to prove almost a new continent for me, since I had been too young to remember much about it when my parents had left there.

For several weeks we enjoyed the Calcutta atmosphere of leisure, while Cap spent hours daily with officials, listing the number of cartridges and counting them against the number we had brought into India at Bombay. We had not fired one, so there were no difficulties on that score. Sometimes I went with Cap and assured officials that our enterprise was quite simple, demonstrating that it is possible to earn a way around the world, and that a girl can drive a car many seemingly impossible places for the first time the feats have been attempted.

It was hard to leave Calcutta; there were so many new fine friends to be left behind. But I did go out in a blaze of glory, for I was given the prize at a masquerade ball the night before our boat sailed for Penang. My ayah draped me in a jade green silk sari bordered with silver. I needed no make-up, for my usually fair skin was weathered to the bronze of a high-caste East Indian. I darkened my hair with oriental kohl, hung myself with anklets and bangles, and even managed to fasten on a gold nose stud to complete the illusion of nationality.

Sometime during that evening of the dance, a mosquito or some other insect bit my foot, and the result of that bite was to keep me in Penang long after the scheduled time for leaving. I had an enforced vacation.

Penang proved an ideal island of the Straits Settlements in which to be ill. I chose to live with a Malayan family some distance from Georgetown, which is the capital city. Penang is off the west coast of the Malay Peninsula, and has been under the British flag since sometime in the 1700s.

There was a sandy cove near the camp site and along the beach lay the brown ribbon of coconut husks which make the tropical tidemarks the world over. Back in the forest of towering coconut palms I had found a friend, a lovely young native woman who looked like a living sculpture done in shades of tan. I lingered day after day in the shade of her thatched home and watched her little young husband riding the surf in a big canoe, sometimes fishing and sometimes diving. My mosquito bitten foot had now become very painful. On the board from Calcutta—a small trading vessel—I had sought out the doctor aboard and asked him if he thought the angry spot should be lanced.

"It'll be all right," he assured me, then put on some salve and a bandage and told me it was silly to worry over an insect bite like that.

But I did worry, for when I left the ship I could barely limp along. Cap had to hire a driver for the second car to get it to the garage. The day after I had met my Malay friend I could not stand up without the aid of a stick on which to lean. Mahafi, gay in her purple sarong, went to the town with a message to Cap, and when he saw the ominous green core in the sore on my foot he was horrified.

"I'll settle that doctor," Cap muttered, but of course the small vessel had sailed off for other islands several days before.

Late in the evening Cap returned, bringing with him an old man whom he had found in the native town. The hotel people had recommended the queer practitioner as having been formerly a well-known European physician; it was said he never failed to cure just such troubles as mine.

"There's just one thing I know of to save that leg," the tattered-looking old gentleman said, and I could smell his sodden, whiskey-laden breath as he spoke. He was preparing to lance my foot with a razor blade that he made sterile in a candle flame. He gave Cap instructions for getting a solution of Epsom salts and glycerine.

"If," mumbled the old fellow again, "that does not take the poison all out and get the inflammation down—well—"

I was left to think what it might be like to go through life with one leg missing! I thought I had rather die; but we continued to pour the solution on my foot and I tried not to worry, but to enjoy the exotic tropical island, lush from its frequent rains, while Mahafi, gay in her many-hued sarongs and jasmine-garlanded hair, cared for me as though I were a baby.

My foot was well before the time came for us to visit Saigon in French Indo-China. Saigon is just like any European city; it was from there that we traveled inland and through the jungle country to take part in a tiger shoot. I even found time to be photographed beside the only elephant skull known to have been found in these jungles, all that was left of a long-dead mammoth. It was in Saigon that a young French naval officer presented me with a baby leopard which, of course, I could not carry with me.

Then we went to Angkor, the ancient ruined city of Cambodia that all world tourists know. This is called Angkor Thom, while the city and temple, Angkor Wat, lie a short distance to the south. Near here we photographed an Annamite girl with her black lacquered teeth which is a fashion that makes even an otherwise lovely face quite horrible. We watched the world-famed dancers, and wondered why the greater part of the Cambodian population has gathered together in the Mekong valley. Everywhere throughout the land, which seems to be a vast plain, we came upon hundreds of ruined temples, smaller but quite as beautiful as Angkor Wat, while we drove the flivvers over massive stone bridges so solidly built that neither flood nor hundreds of years of battering by storm and the floating debris of tree trunks carried down the rivers from inundated areas, have as much as shaken their tremendous foundations. It was in Cambodia, too, that we saw angry poisonous reptiles, and once one of the famed "white" elephants, which are really a sort of dirty gray-pink in color.

It would have been good to linger here but Singapore lay ahead, then Hong Kong and Shanghai, and the long drive we planned through China to reach Mukden.

We boarded a small trading vessel for the mainland, where we would strike the road that led to Singapore. It was as we sailed in this that I remembered to ask Cap how much the old doctor had charged for cutting my foot.

"A quart of good whiskey was exactly what the old duffer asked for," said Cap, who was a strict teetotaler, and added, "I gave him a gallon—your cure was worth that, I guess and the sooner the old fellow drinks himself out of the gutter he has got himself down to, the better for him. I wonder who he was."

"Cap!" I exclaimed, and then thought maybe Cap was right. That poor old doc! Something put him down one day and he never got up—with the wide world so beautiful it seemed a shame for men to go that way.

The road to Singapore was exciting; we saw snakes by the side of it, and monkeys shrieked and jabbered at us until my heart ached for small Chango. He had been left in Calcutta with a lovely mem-sahib whose pet had died, and who immediately loved my monkey. We traveled at night for coolness and I kept my bumper close to the taillight of Cap's car for there was the muffled roar of tigers reaching us from the jungles. When day broke I stopped and found red lichee fruit to gather from bushes at the roadside, and we made coconuts our daily bread.

It was sunset as we reached the great naval base; Singapore harbor was dotted with Malayan fishing boats, and Dutch traders and British merchantmen and navy cruisers were laying at anchor. Singapore welcomed us with headlines. I became a guest in a stately mansion, played tennis on superb courts, and Cap battled with officialdom so that we might take the cars into China at Shanghai. It appeared there was a first-class war going on in Northern China, and my unwary announcement to a newspaper reporter that we intended to drive through to Mukden caused us endless delay.

At last we were aboard the Albert Voegler, bound for Shanghai. On this small vessel we steamed into the broad mouth of the Yangtze Kiang. The muddy stream swirled under torrential rain; the water boiled at the sides of the ship and a heavy mist hung tenaciously over the swollen current. The vessel just crawled into sight of Shanghai's twentieth-century sky-line and we could barely see it through the fog-laden atmosphere. At the wharf a hundred brown, claw-like hands sought to drag us almost bodily to the waiting rickshaws. Rain continued to pour, and rickshaw men jostled each other for fares. We wanted to get to the post office quickly, for mail was due. I caught my breath and hung on for dear life to the rickshaw side-handles. I had fleeting glimpses of Cap, and saw he had a stranglehold on the straps also. I stared at the stooping back and rippling muscles of the coolie pulling me; his blue pajamas were rolled above his knees, exposing bulging, knotted muscles in his legs. We traveled at an incredible speed as the man made dexterous twists and turns, and I kept my balance with difficulty as he dashed round a corner, while occasionally he shouted a long drawn out, "Ah-ah-ah-ah!" to scatter the pedestrians.

I arrived at the post office, but Cap was before me and there was no mail. There had been, it seemed, but where the letters had gone to no one seemed to know. We sought out sub-post offices, then went to the shipping agents and to the hotels. Our letters had vanished, and I was bitterly disappointed. The tears stung my eyes, for I had counted on hearing from mother. All my grown-up self-sufficiency seemed to disappear.

We returned to the riverfront and put the cars through Customs, but no amount of persuasion would release us the sports rifles and ammunition. We simply had to have the rifles along, but by now I had learned all there is to know of official dilatoriness. Embassies and consulates seem to want to move heaven and earth so that they may find a certain tint of paper on which to write a certain type of note; and then, maybe, the ink does not match.

We went to the American consulate and found the Consul, who was a big, friendly man. He calmed us down, and glory of glories, our mail was in the consular offices.

Then he called his wife and she made a tea party for me and the newspapermen came in. We had certainly got off on the right foot in Shanghai. We were forced to keep office hours at the display room of our favorite make of car, while they took in our muddied, battered but still stream-lined automobiles and promised them an expert overhauling in readiness for the North. Our meeting places and film-lectures were correspondingly crowded, while the Consul's wife mothered me and all hardships receded in my memory, so that the old conquering spirit came welling to the surface.

India was now scratched off the route map, and an arrow was sketched in which pointed to Peiping, Tientsin and Mukden; and that Mukden adventures were to lead to the first automobile drive across the Portuguese East African jungle was something unknown as yet, but in the stars. Everything became more exciting as our tour progressed.

We Become Tough

SHANGHAI was just another half-dozen pages turned in my diary when we reached Tientsin on the way to Peiping and Mukden.

"You cannot continue," officials in Tientsin assured us. "Ahead of you are floods, famine, banditry and civil war."

"I wish," I said to Cap, "someone would have an encouraging word just once—it seems to me that officials always think in negatives."

Already we had seen evidence of flood; the streets in the lower section of the city were blockaded to prevent the rising water from sweeping over the Russian concession. We were convinced that smaller river bridges were swept away, and the larger crowded to capacity with refugees from the fighting and the overwhelming waters.

"But, gentlemen, we must go ahead; we must reach Peiping. We cannot possibly afford to remain here longer, and we will not turn back."

The officials shook graying heads; the madness of Americans was beyond their comprehension. Very well, it was our own risk; and the papers were duly endorsed, but they insisted that we take a man along with us to act as guide and interpreter. A White Russian mechanic working at the Tientsin garage where our cars were undergoing one of their periodic overhaulings, was being transferred to Peiping, so when it developed that he knew many Chinese dialects, everyone was satisfied to have him go with us, even the officials. The Russian had transportation to Peiping and we had our guide. He knew his way; he knew, fairly well, how to handle the natives we met, but he was rather helpless as a pioneering tourist.

A four-inch coating of dust on the road out of Tientsin lasted for twenty miles, then on the twenty-first mile we slid into a soft and slimy bog that finally forced us to drive atop the broad and ancient dikes which in many places the Chinese had converted into cemeteries. At places we had difficulty in passing, for some of the coffins lay open to the weather, and the skeleton was to be seen inside.

Our speed was less than walking pace, so our progress was slow, and incredible difficulties began to crop up. I watched ahead and saw the trail lead up a sloping bank of another dike, and there make an abrupt left turn before the summit was reached. I raced the engine of my car, which made an heroic effort to take the grade, but the turn finished us. The rear wheels were spinning furiously on the muddy slope. I tried to warn Cap but was not in time, and his car had the same fate, but on a lower level.

The Russian ran to the edge of the trail and hailed laborers from a paddy field. They came running readily, eager to give all the help they could. It was my first close-up of the poorer peasants and I stared frankly at their burnt sienna skin, the black slits which were eyes, and the flattened elongation which made an embryo nose. Their faces were ugly to American eyes, but their expressions were kindly.

Now two tow ropes were fastened to the chi-chu, and as the patient coolies harnessed themselves to the task, I counted the ribs in their half-starved bodies. They commenced to hum a low melodious chant, dug their toes into the mud and sand, and the cars began to move upward slowly to the higher level.

From my car's supply compartment I produced chocolates, many boxes of which I had been given by Shanghai friends; we had no rice with which to pay the coolies, and so we offered the sweets. The guide tried in vain to explain what ch0ocolate was, but at last I captured one young boy by the nape of the neck and forced a bit of chocolate between his teeth. At first his terror was uncontrollable; his muscles stiffened, his eyes rolled, he gurgled in his throat—and then a change came which would have proved a fortune as an advertising picture for some chocolate manufacturer: That coolie boy relaxed, swallowed and smiled. He uttered a barrage of Chinese superlatives to describe this thrice-blessed taste to his brother coolies; he held out his hand for more chocolates, and we left the poor devils licking their scrawny, smeared fingers. I looked back at them taking up their work again on the level, uninteresting fields, so different from the lush cultivation of flowers, fruit and vegetables we had seen round Shanghai.

An hour later we had reached a village, and Cap was quoting a verse from his favorite Buddha, "To keep the body in good health is a duty, for otherwise we shall not be able to trim the lamp of wisdom and keep our minds strong and clear," while he set up the camera, and recorded on the loveliest things of China: its hospitality to the stranger.

Night had compelled a halt in our hard travel, and the appearance of a small village seemed an answer to prayer. We stopped on the outskirts, then drove slowly between low, primitive homes built of stubble and mud. The street was sunken, worn with the traffic of hundreds of years. Impish youngsters peered at us, while every now and then there would appear in a door opening a woman who emptied slops into the street.

"Chi-chu, chi-chu!" shrieked a pack of children who seemed to spring from the mud under our wheels. They were stark naked. We moved more slowly to avoid touching them, and now we had time to see the brown faces of men and women who had come to stare. I was horror-stricken at the signs of indescribable suffering and patient endurance.

We noticed the abundant hair of the men, none of whom had a short hair cut; and we were just as much interested in the lack of hair among the women, some of whom had coquettishly tied little cloth "buns" to their bald scalps. Later I enquired about this, and was told the baldness comes from plastering the hair to the scalp with grease. As brides, the women have the coiffure correctly done according to traditional mode, then as long years of labor follow, with childbearing and work in the fields, the new growth of hair, or strands of hair which have come loose, are simply glued back upon the old, and then all of the hair comes out. There were some traces of foot-binding in this village, and we watched women hobbling in tiny wooden slippers. Since the peasants are not accustomed to binding the feet I was curious about these women, but found out nothing.

The head man of the village brought food to us at the elevated spot beyond the main street where we had spread tarpaulins. There were bowls of rice and green tea served in blue glazed pots. I produced ivory chopsticks from my kit, and the audience watched me eating while they nodded approval of my accomplishment, and batted their fans against their hands.

China became my tutor in philosophy, for I never saw a Chinese betray surprise, chagrin or resentment, and they seem inured to disappointment; yet there is a sense of hopefulness about them, or perhaps it is more a certainty of things coming right.

Exhilaration caught me again as we arrived in Peiping, for we had surmounted one more barrier to our progress. As we rode through the dust-covered streets of this center of government, as it was then, I began to forget difficulties under the influence of the inevitable headlines. I had another record: first Paris to Peiping chauffeuse. That was always exciting.

But before we experienced these things, we had adventures of differing kinds. Not far from the entrance to Peiping—maybe thirty or forty miles—we hit a road which was a remnant of the ancient glory of China. This highway had originally been built of stone flags, and at periodic intervals there had been marble bridges. But the glory was gone, for the flags were broken and many missing. We came to a toll post that marked a province boundary, and stopped so that a soldier might inspect our baggage. Beyond this place the dike on which we were traveling ended in a washout so we portaged the supplies to the other side of the yawing gap, but when I shouldered a gasoline can to do my share, I made a misstep and found myself up to the waist in quicksand. The guide was near and he grabbed my arm; I struggled, sank further, and then, when it seemed my effort was spent, the Russian found a splintered board and with its aid got me up to the firmer surface. That gave me a fright, and I sat in the car while the Russian went back to find coolies to help us. With this native help we circled around the washout in the empty cars, and got them backed up to the pile of supplies. Then we camped for the night, utterly exhausted, I from the scare in the quicksand more than from the work.

I really thought then we would never see Peiping, for daylight brought no stop to our difficulties. We came on an old marble bridge, with arch and balustrades sculptured in real beauty of design, but the disjointed flags over the single span were twisted, the heavier stones sunk to the foundation, and the smaller left jutting out. There seemed no hope of driving across, for the bridge approach was sunken, and what was left of the marble was a step higher than the actual road bed.

"Maybe we can find a ford," said Cap, and we spent hours clambering up and down the banks of the stream, which was swollen and raging in a torrent.

"I'm going to jump the incline," I said to the guide, thinking I could make the attempt before Cap returned from his survey, for I was sure he would veto my trying such a thing. I emptied my car of supplies, backed and raced the motor in a low gear, then drove hard ahead. There came a smashing jolt, the car frame quivered and a tire exploded with a shrieking bang; but the front wheels kept on the edge of the bridge while I felt the rear wheels spin in churning sand. Then there came a second bump and I had the whole car on the bridge.

"If you did it, I suppose I can," said Cap gloomily, for he had come running when he heard the tire burst. His car made the gap, and the tires held, but it was that stunt which brought a worse difficulty before we reached Peiping. Then the crankshaft broke when Cap was forcing his car over a sandhill, and it was necessary for me to tow it from there to the city gates.

Soldiers stopped us at the tunnel entrance through the great Tartar bastions that surround Peiping. The men looked half asleep in their coats tied like sacks of meal about the middle.

"On the staff of Wu Pei Fu," shouted the guide, knowing Peiping then to be a hotbed of Central armies; but while two soldiers held tight to the car sides, others ran back to their shelters to fetch officers. It did not seem good to us.

"Step on it," shouted Cap, who was steering the car behind, and I threw mine into gear, starting slowly because of the weight behind. An officer dashed out and charged at me with a drawn saber; it struck the hood of the moving car, and the momentum of the machine tore the weapon from his grasp. I looked back and saw Cap battering over the knuckles the luckless soldier who still clung to the side of his car. Cap was using a tire tool for the purpose. No trouble ever came of our rough entry, and we did not bring the subject up.

Peiping was swarming with humanity: rickshaw coolies; men and women and children; caravans of Mongolians with camels coming in from the Gobi desert; and everywhere soldiers — mercenaries, we were told. Yet this center of China got me by the heartstrings. I do not know why, any more than do many others who, once they live in China, do not wish to leave. Up around Peiping I did not find the country either beautiful or fragrant, for there was pulverized dust and reeking odors and at times horrific downpours of rain. The rivers are yellow, and I did not see a luxuriant valley; maybe to the Occidental it is the pull of centuries piled one on top of the other which constitutes the fascination.

But dust, unpleasant odors and bad roads readily went out of my mind when I found myself in a European bed between the white linen sheets of the Hotel de Pekin, after I had soaked in a tub of hot water.

Each morning I dawdled when I awoke. Always some one had sent me flowers and fruit, and the amah brought me the local newspapers. I was filled with pride and conceit when I read the headlines:

> Seventeen-Year Old Girl Meets
> Adventure in Thirty-Seven Countries.
> Drives from Paris to Peiping.

So it went until the whole story of the exploring party was told, as far as we had gone.

We dined with new-found friends and were entertained at teas by those who wanted to meet us personally. I made real friends among the white women and some of the wives of wealthy Chinese, and greater love has no woman for her sister than they showed, for they threw wide the doors of their wardrobes so that I might borrow dresses to wear to the formal functions for which I had no fit clothing, carrying now only necessities. We attended a Mandarin banquet with courses which numbered well over a score; we enjoyed the deliciousness of roast whole pork, and almond tea which proved just liquid enough to drink. I met Meilin Fong, the noted Chinese dancer, and a dozen notables of the Far East.

But all this social life was on the surface; under it we had a persisting query. We must get to Mukden, and the question was from where should we get passport visas. Soviet Russia was then unrecognized by China, which meant there was no Russian representative within the legation enclosures. There were Soviet representatives in the Chinese city, so we penetrated there, but we came away empty-handed. What seemed the only chance left was in a remark of a clerk. He told Cap that Kharakan was in Peiping.

I left the whole thing to Cap. It seemed wiser that a girl should not appear until everything was arranged, but in the end it was I who secured the visas. When Kharakan went out in a recent Russian purge, I thought of a narrow Chinese street, two importunate Americans and a very courteous Slav.

I Get a Companion

Punctuality each day, going from the Chinese city where his offices were to the place he lived. The ideal meeting place was a narrow street, and before the distinguished man was due to come there, we had no difficulty in lining up our cars so that they blocked the passage of other traffic. I sat by Cap in the rear car, and waited, it seemed, for hours but it was barely ten minutes.

Kharakan was sitting back in the tonneau of his open car when he saw the blockaded street, and gave his chauffeur a sharp order. There was no space in which the car could turn. I was primed and ready. I did not wait for Cap's whispered, "Now!" I sprang to the running board of the big touring car, and saluted the occupant smartly. As concisely as I could, and speaking French, I asked the indulgence of a visa for Siberia.

Kharakan had risen to his feet in surprise at my audacity. He was a tall man with a neatly trimmed black beard. He wore a low felt hat and a long black overcoat. I met his glance with friendly eyes, and he smiled in relief that I was not an assassin. My idea that a girl's plea would work where a man's would fail, was the right one.

"Very well," the Russian said, when I had replied to a string of rapid-fire questions as to our purpose. "Come to my office tomorrow," and he named an hour. I was thankful that he understood French, and Cap was jubilant at my success when we steered the cars out of the way of traffic again.

Olga came next, and although it was Cap who got her to join our expedition for a time, she had really been my discovery. It was while riding early to a luncheon party in the Legation enclosure that I glimpsed Olga for the first time. She was seated on the tilted cushion of a private rickshaw, her face shaded by a large hat, but her crossed legs exposed an enticing length of sheer silk hose.

"What gorgeous legs!" I exclaimed and Cap who was with me, muttered: "Humdinger!"

I was a good deal surprised when a smartly dressed and young-looking woman appeared at the Hotel de Pekin in response to our advertisement for an interpreter and a woman companion to travel with me to Siberia. This woman had an exquisite pair of oblique blue eyes in a face of rather startling pallor; as my glance dropped to her very smart shoes, I knew this was the "humdinger" of the rickshaw. There was no mistaking those legs.

Olga was not old, but there were deep lines about her mouth; yet her eyes were free of crow's feet. She puzzled me, for she would smile with her lips while her eyes remained expressionless; afterward I was to think Olga was a human being out of whom the soul had gone although the body lived. She was the second White Russian we had met, and the first woman of her kind, a victim of the Red Revolution. She told me she had been the wife of a Tsarist officer, and had gone to a concentration camp with others widowed in one of the mass killings. There the helpless crowds of them were left to starve, so that inhibitions broke down and those who died provided sustenance for those who lived. Olga's infant son died.

She told all this in the same monotonous tone, speaking a mixture of English and Polish, but without inflection and apparently without emotion. She told me, after Cap had gone, that she had bought indulgences with her body from a Commandant who had visited the starving creatures in the camp, so had managed an escape to China. She wanted to reach Mukden very badly, but we never found out why, nor did she give any hint of why she agreed to identify herself with our expedition. It fitted in, though, for we needed a Russo-Chinese interpreter, and I really wanted a woman companion. No one else applied for the hazardous journey by road which it was bound to be. So Olga came along, and it was from her I learned my smattering of Russian.

We could not have done without her, for we found sixteen pages of questionnaire to be filled in before the Soviet office representatives would give us Siberian visas, even though we had the ear of Kharakan and wanted to penetrate no further than Vladivostok to embark for Japan. All the time officials and friends prophesied real danger for us in the fighting zones. I was terrified privately and thrilled at the same time. We outfitted Olga in a traveling uniform similar to my own, which she donned quite unperturbed. She assured us she knew several of the North China dialects and felt she could talk us out of difficulties with the soldiery. We did not take into account the mercenary bandits.

Headlines in the Peiping papers, as startling as those which had greeted us in the North China Star, heralded our departure: "Daring young girl to drive over battlefields to Mukden; thence to Japan and the United States—a thousand bandits menace journey." It read alarmingly. In the same paper was a full-page advertisement that Marshal Chang Tso Lin of Mukden offered cash payment to Peiping forces who would desert and join up with his troops. He quoted the exact sums to be paid for a general or a private, and the ranks between, while bonuses were offered for a squad, a troop or a regiment which might be brought along. An aviator fetched a near fortune, and the fortune doubled if the man owned an airplane. The whole thing seemed a bit like opera bouffe. But at the same time American and British gunboats were steaming into Tientsin to evacuate nationals, and in Peiping the exodus toward Nanking was foreshadowed. On our last afternoon in Peiping, I went to a temple and paid homage to a marble god of war. I thought I ought to.

There was a flooded plain stretching beyond the city. Olga rode with me and the cars groaned with their extra supplies of gasoline and tires. The track became worse; holes and fissures filled with mud and filth menaced our progress, which was a snail's pace at best. At last Olga took the wheel and I volunteered to walk a length of yards ahead; if I forded a pool in which the water was no higher than my hips, I signaled the cars on and point out as best I could the worst spots to be avoided, but we had to be pushed and hauled out of more than a score of these quagmires.

Small groups of soldiery were stationed at isolated villages, the majority of them insolent and bullying toward us. "Who gave you the right?" was their stock question. We were delayed for hours while they put down Olga's replies, laboriously scrawling hieroglyphics backward across rice paper.

As we were getting away from one particularly irritating inquisition, a soldier shouted to us to halt after we had the engines running again. Cap was already ahead. I was driving my car, and answered this new challenge with a burst of speed. The soldier ran in pursuit, fumbling to loosen his Mauser so I gave the wheel to Olga, and hung out of the car. I looked over the top of the canvas and made the most horrible face I could. It was a specialty of a face which I had perfected in boarding school. The soldier stopped, flabbergasted. He had heard of foreign devils, no doubt, but this was the first time he was seeing one in the flesh. The same face-making accomplishment was to stand me in good stead a few days later, and also in other countries, but even with it we were taken prisoner outside the next village.

It was one of the poorest of many poor villages we had seen. There was not a human being in sight not a scraggly chicken, not even one of the innumerable mongrel dogs—

wonks, they call them—that are like the pariahs in India eking out a precarious existence by eating slop. We had hoped for food and tea, but we could rouse no one at the huts.

We drove on disappointed; then about a quarter of a mile beyond the last hovel an ominous hiss from my tires told me I had a puncture. I was not prepared to find two wheels flat, the rims sticking firmly into the heavy mud. I looked ahead and saw Cap had stopped. I watched him get down and examine the wheels of his car before he walked back where Olga and I stood helplessly staring at a rusty nail protruding from my right front tire; I could only suppose the other tire had picked up something of the same kind, but I was taken aback at Cap's announcement:

"What's the matter, Aloha—not flats? I've picked up a puncture in one of my back tires."

And just then soldiers descended upon us. They must have been concealed in the mud huts, and why they had let us get so far beyond the settlement I do not know. There were ten of the men, uncouth and rough looking.

Olga addressed the leader, calling him Commandant. He was a fat, furious-looking little man with blood-shot eyes, who strutted and preened himself, and issued orders in a very loud voice. He pretended not to understand what was said, then stuttered out an amazing tirade of which Olga was only able to understand scraps. He accused us of being spies, but for what party or country it was never made clear. He ordered our cars to be pushed to the side of the road, and although we protested against their being moved with flat tires, he was obdurate, and became terribly enraged and batted at soldiers with the flat of his sword to hurry them to their task of harnessing shaggy Manchurian ponies to pull the automobiles from where they were.

The cars were brought to the village, and unceremoniously Olga and I were thrust into a dark and filthy mud hut, while the flat door, which seemed to be all of one piece of wood, was fastened securely on the outside.

There was no window, but we could hear Cap's protesting voice rising higher as he shouted in English, German, Polish, and a mixture of all three, and we knew something was going on but we could not quite make out what. Later Cap told us he thought the officer understood some English, for when Cap had demanded by words and signs that some of the soldiers help him to change and patch the tires, and then blow them up, they had received orders to do so.

The air in our hovel was foul and I was feeling sick when the door opened noisily and two soldiers pushed forward with tea and rice which they carried in bowls. Olga spoke again, using several dialects, but the men turned faces that were blank and brutish in the half light and answered nothing. When we had eaten, they lifted the empty vessels and went out. They made no move to molest us. Olga and I planned on shifts of watching and sleeping during the night, and of course we had the little revolvers on our persons well concealed, but we had not been searched. The thought of those weapons was comforting, but I could not sleep because I was panicky about Cap's fate, and now all was quiet on the outside. I tried the rough board door, but it would not move; then I planted myself with my back and head resting against the mud and stubble wall, my feet straight out before me. I may have dozed but I did not sleep, for the night was taken up with scratching. The vermin was appalling.

Cap was at the door when the soldiers opened it in the morning and again pushed the bowls of tea and rice at us, but this time we were summoned before the Commandant.

"You'll have to do some swell talking," said Cap to Olga. "I've been practically all night showing the old boy our photos. If we'd had electricity we might have shown the films and convinced him that our ways are not evil. I've waved the American flag under his nose—the old buzzard knows what it is all right, don't think he doesn't—now it's up to you, Olga."

But the fate of our release lay in my hands after all. Olga talked, then I came forward holding more photographs and some of the North China Star clippings with which there was a full page of illustrations. I had just started to spread this before the officer when the man seized my wrists and began to shake and shiver as though he had an ague. I thought the beast was about to throttle me in his rage, for his face was purple and swollen under the yellow stretched skin, his eyes were starting from his head, and saliva was drooling from his gaping mouth. I tugged myself free from his dirty hands which had slackened their grip; then he reeled and fell. It was a stroke, of course. He was quite dead when Cap rushed forward and the confusion among the nine or ten soldiers of his company was truly awful.

"Run for the cars," said Cap, and Olga and I rushed out and made for the machines on the open space where they stood. None of the soldiers attempted to stop us, and we jolted along the roadway, got safely by the mud pits in which we had picked up the nails and soon were headed straight north.

It was an unpleasant interlude, and we felt relief when we began to pass columns of troops moving in our direction. They scattered always before our advancing cars. Their equipment was nondescript, the things which we noticed most being the big paper umbrellas which each carried, and the quilted overcoats too long for each man's height, so that the garments trailed in mud puddles as the men dragged along. They did not seem able to march. A German rifle jiggled like the guitar of a bedraggled troubadour from a string thrown over the back, and officers rode shaggy Mongolian ponies and tagged along by the ragged columns. Then it rained, and we watched waves of the men seeking shelter through fields of long grass. There were some sturdy ponies that hauled carts with wooden wheels studded with spikes, and on the carts were supplies and guns. The Chinese soldier carries nearly all he needs, with his straw mat wrapped round the paper umbrella and hanging from his tightened cartridge belt a tin pot for tea and a bowl to hold his chow, while somewhere about his person he stows chopsticks and tobacco.

At last we saw telegraph poles ahead. That meant Mukden, but before we reached it we had to cross the actual fighting zone. We heard the booming of cannon, the faint rattle of machine guns. I recognized these things, and my childhood memories flashed back with all the horrors of war, and of the field at Ypres where my father still lies.

We reached a railroad with the highway running parallel to it, so that we saw boxcars laden with men for gun fodder. We stopped to outline our plan of approach through the opposing lines, and found a young soldier who spoke excellent English. He had been in the States, and it seemed that he understood our exploring enterprise. He warned us of barbed-wire entanglements, and then a small gratuity in silver brought us the information that the sector of level ground where the armies fought was without a barrier.

It was no man's land from this point on, and the whole thing was pretty dreadful, enough to make me an ardent advocate of settlement of political and economic disputes by talk instead of bullets. Bodies lay sprawled on the ground in advanced stages of putrefaction and the stench nauseated us; some bodies were shattered with shell, and others lay as though they had been sucking some rank water from the ditch to ease burning throats and lungs.

"Gas," said Cap laconically, "or small arms fires," when I questioned him later on the bodies which had lain apparently unmutilated; but Cap did not want to talk of what he had seen.

It seemed that we had crossed the danger zone in safety when a group of officers stopped us. It was as if they had come up from underground, so sudden was their appearance. Cap had already halted and was showing credentials when Olga and I came up. The men were quite polite, but they rode in the cars with us and directed our progress. We came to the suburbs of Mukden, and I was told to stop my car before a long, rambling, European-style house. The Chinese officers, courteous still, bade us enter the doorway. We waited inside, and then a white man entered the reception hall where we were. He wore khaki shorts, a neat white shirt and a pale blue sleeveless pull-over sweater. The right sleeve of his shirt hung limp and empty at his side.

"Americans, eh? Well, I'm sort of running the show here—Sutton is my name." His voice was pleasantly cultivated and his manner friendly.

"Fortunate they brought you here," he went on. "They've a bad habit of going direct to the native staff sometimes, and that means an insalubrious prison if they suspect you of spying."

We told of our recent experience in the apparently deserted village. "Lucky for you the Lord struck the old chap when he did," was the comment.

I stared at General Sutton open-mouthed, frankly full of curiosity. This was the famed—or notorious—General Sutton, depending on how one cared to consider those things. When he looked at me directly, I turned my eyes to the trophies of war and the hunt that decorated the walls of the long room to which he had led us. Cap told our story and explained the purpose of our exploring expedition.

"I'll hold a strong personal interest in you while you are in Mukden." Thus General Sutton relieved our anxiety, and I had infinite faith in this ex-officer of the British Army. Stories about him were fabulous; he was accused of inciting the Chinese Civil War, some said he was Chang Tso Lin's right-hand man, and others said he controlled an arsenal in Mukden. I knew him as a most charming and generous host.

Servants now brought in drinks; a silver Russian samovar steamed and whistled.

"In your honor." The General inclined his head toward Olga, who had kept silent since we arrived, although she spoke and understood English as well as her native Russian.

"You will be free to go anywhere you wish in Mukden— I shall be seeing you," said the General as he saw us into the cars again. The Chinese officers and soldiers had disappeared and small yellow servitors stood guard by the muddied cars. Some magic certainly worked for us, for late in the afternoon Cap received a call from the small European Club of Mukden and asked if I would give a film-lecture before the members.

On the Road to Vladivostok

OLGA left us in Harbin, where a member of the European colony offered her a good position. I had enjoyed her companionship, over the long, tortuous plains of northeastern Manchuria which we had crossed by car, for Olga was charming. Good fortune was with us. General Sutton, who, after our first lecture at the European Club, had toted us bodily back to his home in Mukden to sample major hospitality. We secured rich loot in new films in Mukden, with types of Tartars, Mongols, Chinese and Manchus. We prowled over the city unhindered by officialdom, and stood at times on the wall to look down on one side at ancient collections of filth, houses of clay, narrow twisting alleys hollowed deep by a constant stream of camels and donkeys, sweating under too heavy loads; on the other side of the wall, controlled by Japanese, was a clean and modern town. The Mukden railway station belonging to Japan is built on a grand scale, making it the hub of a wheel, with the streets like spokes leading out from the center.

General Sutton gave us the freedom of his home.

"Stay here," he said hospitably, so that was how, in the Sutton arsenal, I fired a trench mortar. The horrible little steel barrels on tripods, three- and six-inch, were being tested. I watched the soldiers trying out a new batch of shells, then they let me pick up one, shove it into the mouth of the barrel and jump back. There came an ear-shattering boom, the gun leaped in its emplacement, and the shell shrieked into the air. It was bound for a target a mile and three-quarters distant. Any one of these shells might have exploded in the barrel.

But in a month we were well on the way to Harbin. We slept in Chinese inns on the way, and we ate dozens of hard-boiled eggs of a doubtful youth. The cold was becoming intense when the sun did not shine, and we made hard going of many river fords. Once we boarded a ferry and small boys punted us to the further side. We ate eggs, the muddy water stank, and chunks of thin ice floated in it with gobs of filth and dead animals. Cap broke the shell of an egg and a boiled chicken popped to view. Cap was awfully sick, but the hunger-ridden eyes of our ferry lads begged for the boiled dreadfulness, so we bestowed largesse of all the eggs we had left.

Harbin was flourishing; gay little shops lined the muddy, cobbled, wide thoroughfare. The city seemed a bit of western Russia set down beside the Sungari River in China. Old Harbin remains China; new Harbin is like old Russia. At the south end of the main avenue a wooden church reared onion-shaped cupolas against the hard sky. Russian refugees, wrapped in rags and somber melancholy, obviously were being made to feel like intruders, but there was no place else for them to go. Loving travel with new sights, new sounds and new lands, Cap and I discussed what it must be like to wander the world knowing there was no land one dared call one's own. For us, no matter where we were, there was always, beyond one ocean or the other, America.

It was a relief to start on the road to Vladivostok. Our guide from the Sutton entourage turned back, and with Cap in the lead again, our cars traveled parallel with the track of the Manchurian railroad. The path was a mere trail broken by peasants' carts, the going difficult and the pace a crawl, with the thermometer dropping steadily. Mr. Ostroumoff, general manager of the railroad in Harbin, was helpful. He arranged that the one freight train going from Harbin each week, and always guarded by an armored car, would stop if we signaled for help; likewise the train which was to come from the other direction.

"Be careful of Chung Hutzee bandits," the general manager said. "You pass through a deep forest."

We had driven more than half a day after entering the Great Black Forest when we ran out of gas. We had hoped to renew our supply at the last fortified farmhouse where we had rested, but they had none, and what we had brought us to the edge of a Mongolian settlement. Cap walked to the village and came back with news of mixed cheer. There was no gas, but the armored freight was expected any minute, and there was sure to be gas at the next station on the line, where the freight coming inland was expected to pass.

I elected to stay in my car covered by two tarpaulins, both of which leaked. I peaked apprehensively through the holes at groups of Mongolians who chattered in their curious language as they came to look at the cars. Then a freak of nature overtook us and a thunderstorm with pelting rain sent the spectators with their shaggy ponies for shelter under the pine trees. The rain changed to sleet, and as the storm grumbled off in the distance the wet earth began to freeze over hard. I sat up, got myself from under the swaddling tarpaulins, looked at the rows of Mongol bystanders, and began to pray that Cap would get back on that freight — and soon.

By the afternoon of the next day we had reached Pogranichnia, the Siberian frontier town. There flags were flying, the multicolors of China, and the crimson-and-gold hammer and sickle of the Soviet. I braced myself to try out my Russian, as Cap waved back a signal to stop.

"Stoi!" said the Siberian guard, coming to a stiff salute. His uniform cap was flat-peaked, his black blouse trimmed with pink, and an ominous pistol sagging his belt down over one hip. He spoke a queer mixture of French and Russian, and I waved to him to approach.

"Tovarish," he called me, then shook hands and seated himself in my car. Ahead was a rambling village, where the customs office was housed in a timbered cabin. We had no trouble; I took out the Soviet courtesy flags we carried, and put them up beside the Stars and Stripes, which looked incongruous. This no doubt was a breach of diplomatic etiquette, for our country did not then recognize the Soviet government—something which brought difficulties later—but it smoothed the immediate way. Farmer *mujiks* crowded around the cars and asked questions of us. Most of them seemed to have relatives in the United States; they felt abused when we did not have personal knowledge of their friends.

Our officer friend remained with us until we reached Vladivostok, but reaching Vladivostok was no sinecure. Cap bought me a pair of fur mittens to wear over my woolen gloves, and my hands continued to become icy cold as I drove, yet it was only early October. The brittle ice surface of the trail broke at times into the bog beneath, leaving knifelike edges sticking up, and we had puncture after puncture in the badly worn tires. There was almost continuous sleet that cut my face and burned like fire. We came to villages surrounded by fences with gates across the roadway. It must have been years since foreigners had passed that way, if ever, for the peasants crowded to stare when we stopped for food, and they followed the cars until we had gone far beyond the stockade.

Just as the gate of the next village I encountered trouble. The front wheel of my car plunged into a hole and buckled badly. Cap towed me into the township, where a mob of fair-haired giants watched the car being jacked up and the disc wheel unscrewed. A huge young man, who saluted gravely, removed his flat-peaked fur cap and spoke quite good English as he directed us to a blacksmith.

"Yes, Tovarish, come this way to the shop, the telegas-maker can fix the wheel of your carriage."

Cap and the Soviet officer, whose name we never learned either to pronounce or write, went to look for food. A huge gray-bearded man seized the car wheel; he looked as though he could reshape it with his bare hands, and I watched the sparks fly from the anvil until Cap fetched me to eat black bread, eggs and sour cream in another izba where there were logs burning in a fireplace, and potted plants were ranged on a bare board table.

The mended wheel traveled well, but the delay had tired me. So it was I went at once to a *gostinitza*, where the innkeeper was an old, white-bearded *mujik* who wore an *armiak* of embroidered cloth. He looked like a reincarnated Boyar. Without stopping to wash, I climbed into the rough bed, minus sheets, that stood in an alcove beyond the main room. The thick atmosphere of pent-up humanity and stove heat penetrated to my retreat, but I slept until I discovered the Siberian bedbug is twice as carnivorous as his kind in other lands.

When we set off in the morning the *mujiks* at the inn waved to us and called, "Do Svidania."

"Good-by," we called out, and said to each other: "We'll make Vladivostok this evening."

Red Colonel with Curls

"TODAY is my eighteenth birthday."

I remember writing those words in my diary in the dreary Hôtel de Versailles in Vladivostok, which appeared to me but the bleached skeleton of a city. My room, at the end of long, dark corridors, boasted on huge bay window with heavy draperies, and a bed curtained off with clumsy burgundy-red plush curtains; there was a rustic table in the middle of the room and hand-hewn chairs. The palatial furnishings had been ransacked in the eighteen revolutions and counter-revolutions the city had experienced. The ugly gloom of the curtains and bed must have saved them from the raiders.

My thoughts flew to my mother and sister, Meg, and I riffled back the pages of the diary I had kept in these two years of travel. I could hardly believe twenty-four months had gone by, and yet I was in my thirty-eighth country since the momentous day when Cap and mother had consented to the enterprise. Two years of adventure—my mind was crowded with experiences which would need volumes to relate, and even then each country would not get its due. There were no words, either, in which I could express the feelings which had grown out of the contact with the queer places of the world. And now I had been for two weeks in this tin-roofed, white-washed Siberian city on the edge of cold desert and cold ocean.

There was no privacy in this hotel. Employees were overwhelmed with curiosity, and came and went in my room at will. I kept close to the shelter of the draped bed to make my morning toilette, for there were no locks on the doors of a government-supervised hostelry. One obeyed the rules and ate the plain two-course meals provided, sans sweets and sans table napkins. Our arrival increased the registered guests in the huge caravanserai to nine, the others seemed to be farmers on an annual trek to the seaport's hops for supplies, and two government men from the west. All of these people, and others, had opened my door at intervals during each day; timidly they held their caps in their hands, looked at me with bland, innocent eyes and said: "Good day, Tovarish!" and retreated as quietly as they had come.

All were courteous, and I became used to these interruptions, so that in the midst of my present rather gloomy cogitations about an elderly eighteen, I was not surprised when the door opened. But I sprang to my feet in some consternation when a very smart Soviet officer strode across the dreary bare waste of my room, saluted and barked out a command. It lost some of the snap, for I could not understand him, since my Russian for the time being was kindergarten in quality. At last, what with his parading up and down the room, snapping to salute and pointing to his watch, I understood I was to report at the Soviet Army parade grounds at three o'clock precisely.

I tried to keep calm but I felt panicky inside. The parade ground is also the place of execution, and I had heard a good deal about so-called trials and their results. I had not seen Cap all day, and I did not know where he was; we did not have a film-lecture to give that day, and the next day was set for our departure for Japan. Meanwhile the officer remained where he was. It was already half past two and the parade grounds were five miles from the town. I had seen the place. I put on my leather helmet.

Two uniformed men received me; they saluted and shook hands with the customary formality. I caught sight of men at a distance, and with them was the Soviet officer who had stuck to us like glue since our arrival in Siberia. We waited; I tried to make conversation in broken Russian in an endeavor to appear calm. I was really terrified, for the whole thing was so mysterious.

A regiment of soldiers arrived, deploying from whitewashed barracks on the hillside and led by a band, the gigantic brass instruments glinting in the sun. They played the "Marseillaise", considerably off key. It was bitterly cold. I watched the tall young handsome soldiers, whose pointed cloth helmets resembled the old German spikers, except for a big red star in front. There were three officers with small sleeve insignia who were much shorter than their men, and thick-set and dark in comparison. One of these was the Commandant. I was motioned to take a position with officers on each side of me and behind. My head buzzed, and then I heard the old familiar whir of our moving-picture camera. Could this be a courtmartial? I had heard of such things. The Commandant spoke:

"Tovarish, Aloha Baker, you are the first girl to drive an automobile to Siberia. I have seen your films and they are very wonderful. We want to commemorate your visit here; you are appointed honorary Colonel in the Third Nihinsky Regiment of Vladivostok." The man was most complimentary.

Until I felt myself dizzy with relief, I had not realized how nearly overcome with fear I had let myself become. There was a harp command, the regiment swung toward me and I stood at attention between the two senior officers.

"Present arms!"

An orderly handed the Commandant a set of sleeve pips. While the lines of rifles were held at their quaint "present arms," with slender rifles and long fixed bayonets pointing toward me, the officer pinned the pips on my coat sleeve and the band played the "Internationale" as a purring obbligato.

It was truly thrilling. What a birthday celebration! I forgave Cap his lack of congratulations when we had a feast of bean soup and black bread in the officers' mess. The Commandant made a speech about the equality of women, and I was the shining illustration.

I had thought my celebration complete, but there was more to come. Mr. Zimmer, whom we had met the first day in Vladivostok, was waiting at the hotel when we returned. He brought an invitation from his mother to come to her house for a birthday feast. Cap, it seemed, had told them about the date.

The Zimmer home looked dilapidated. Whitewashed and tin-roofed as all others in the once flourishing seaport, it faced a cold and desolate street, but inside the house was charming. I marveled at the luxurious Persian rugs on polished floors, a sideboard rich with glassware and silver, high French mirrors reflecting the flames of a log firewhich burned in a wide grate. This was now a bourgeois home.

"The furnishings are cherished remnants of our once elaborate ménage," explained Madame Zimmer, whose kindliness was marked. I rejoiced in the company of several girls of my own age. Chai was served, tall glasses of tea with sweet jam flavoring, and as we drank we chattered in French. The girls had a million questions they wanted answered about the outer world, for they had been to school in Paris. Our other amusement was exploring the contents of a big wooden chest, richly embossed in silver. Wedding veils were in it, and laces and embroideries; heavy silver chains too, and at the bottom lay an evening gown.

"Our great grandmother was as tall as you," exclaimed Sacha, daughter of the house, as she measured this gown from my shoulders. "She was fair, too, only with blue eyes. Do put this dress on—we are all too small to wear it," she added.

I put on the gown, to please myself and to please these generous friends. It was made of China-blue plush with a close fitting bodice, and the wide skirt swept behind into a long train. In the mirror I saw myself a "wilitti" of seventy years before. My hair was bound in curls on top, with ringlets at the side of my head. I glided into the dining room like yesterday's heroine of a Tsarist novel, and I ate of the fifteen-course dinner like an American girl who savored the difference between a spoonful of soy-beans and joints of meat, boiled fish, casserole of salmon, platters of roast goose, smoking hot borstch, caviar, wine and black bread. We were offered the food by peasant servitors walking silently in gray woolen-socked feet. It was a leftover from another Russia.

A silver candelabra gave a mellow light, and the company was increased now by the Commandant, many officers of the regiment and more young women, who spoke English, German, French and often their own melodious Slavic tongue, which I began to follow more easily. We danced, we listened to beautiful music, and then, long after midnight, the world-tour Cinderella discarded her China-blue plus garment, and in high boots, sheepskin coat and the leather Sam Browne over the shoulder of my decorated jerkin, I marched into the darkness of a Russian pre-dawn. General Sutton had had this Sam Browne made for me in his Chinese saddlery and I was very proud of it.

It was with alarm that I discovered there was a blinding blizzard blowing, for we were to sail at noon on a small Japanese ship now riding hard at anchor in the harbor, otherwise practically denuded of shipping.

Our Thirty Ninth Country

THERE had been a simplicity in getting into Siberia which was disarming. Getting out was another matter. We were well aware that some wrong move on our part might change the official attitude from its apparent pleasure in our company, and so we took the advice of Mr. Zimmer to say nothing about leaving until the last possible moment.

We "moseyed" the cars down on the dock.

"Have you the right to leave Siberia?" was the first question.

I hastily put back on my car the Soviet flag which I had been in process of removing. The ship on which we proposed to make our crossing to the land of the Rising Sun was a Japanese one, and I wanted to start the journey tactfully, so the Soviet flag had not seemed one of the best decorations to carry.

"Have you clearance papers for the cars and baggage?"

Fortunately the blizzard had become furious in proportions; because of it high officials had not come to their offices, and minor officials seemed no more keen to keep out in the weather than we were. They wanted to get back to their office shacks and we wanted to get on the freighter.

No tickets sold until one hour before sailing," was the dictum at the steamship agency. Long before the hour limit was reached the skipper found out we had no advance bookings; the customs officer discovered we had no export permit and the Commissar remembered what we sincerely hope he had entirely forgotten—that we had taken photographs which were still uncensored.

Everyone seemed intent on giving us as much trouble as possible. When all obstacles seemed overcome, another would loom up. Now we did not have the pink slip. Someone gave me a piece of pink paper, but it was not signed, and it was no good until it was signed. Mr. Zimmer arrived panting, flustered and battered by the elements; Cap had sent a message to him to come and help us, and he proved a friend in need.

The clerk looked up at us with mild blue eyes:

"The Commissar who signs the pink slip is not coming from his house today because of the blizzard."

I looked at the young individual in stupefaction. It seemed as though we were defeated; even Mr. Zimmer could not command the weather and the Commissar. Then the clerk yawned again—his office was unpleasantly hot with a monster stove roaring; he reached for a pen and signed the pink slip himself.

We had fifteen minutes until noon. I saved up the parting maledictions I should have liked to pour upon that clerk's head; I ran to purchase the tickets, waving the pink slip as I went, and Cap superintended the cars now being lashed securely on the foredeck.

The skipper proved to be very glad of passengers. I climbed to the upper deck and, clinging to a stanchion as support against the gale, I took a last look at the sad panorama of a ghost city wrapped in its winding sheet of driving snow.

"Japan," said Cap, "then Hawaii; but if Japan is really good we can skip the islands and make for Detroit for an overhaul. And Aloha"—he paused with that bit of dramatic effect with which he prefaced important announcements— "there's something come up; I got it in my last mail." He handed me a newspaper story taken from a New York paper. It told, in detail, of a Capetown-to-Cairo highroad, and the story of the road was tacked on to the report of a party of people headed by someone called "Courtreat" who had traveled over part of this road by car. They featured Mrs. "Courtreat."

"But she did not drive herself," said Cap. Of course I knew what was in his mind. I had the Bombay-to-Calcutta record chalked up, and Capetown-to-Cairo would be surely well worth attempting. I thrilled at the thought of another unexpected experience of a continent.

When we reached Tsuruga Bay, Japanese officials wearing black silk uniforms with clanking nickel-plated swords came aboard our freighter. Through their interpreter they questioned us, together and separately dwelling on every phase of our Soviet visit. They were so suspicious that we were forced to camp for six days on the docks at Tsuruga Bay, awaiting an Imperial permit to allow us to travel as an "educational body," across Nippon. It seemed an inauspicious beginning to our thirty-ninth country, but Japan was to surprise us.

I put up the Japanese courtesy flags and we drove inland through a bamboo forest with the lofty leaf-tips meeting overhead. The landscape seemed as familiar as a Japanese print. Our road reached a lake shore at a point opposite Otsu, and we left the cars to photograph some quaint fisher folk. We strolled to a little temple of red and black lacquer encrusted with golden dragons, where a group of small girls stared. I pointed the camera to get a record of pale features and charming figures wrapped in orange and mauve kimonos, then they fled to the temple entrance and peeked at us from between their fingers.

Dusk fell, the sky became silver. On a solitary junk the crimson sail flapped a bit in the coming night wind. The whole scene was lovely.

"Let's camp here," said I, and Cap was ready to agree when a tall young Japanese, in a neat brown kimono, approached us. He held out his hand to Cap. Western fashion:

"How do you do," he said in excellent English. "You are the Americans the Kobe papers wrote about, coming this way from Europe and Asia?"

Cap nodded. He had no chance to speak, for the voluble stranger was telling us he had been reared in California— "but I now remain in the village of my forefathers."

There was no inn in the village, and our host was horrified that we should think of camping.

"My wife does not speak English, but our home is yours for the night; come now and have tea with us." Of course we accepted; this was a rare chance to see a real Japanese home.

Our host seemed to be well-to-do; the house was large and low, and made of bamboo slats and oiled paper. Stepping stones led through a landscaped garden and we left our shoes on the last one before we entered the house. Our hostess was delightful, and I felt a giantess beside her dainty four feet of height, which was wrapped in a dark blue kimono, with an under one of mauve showing at the sleeves. She had a broad obi in light blue round her petite middle, but my masculine outfit intrigued her as much as hers did me. We became friends immediately.

Each of the four rooms which we saw had one solid wall and three made to slide. The solid wall had a recess with a dais which is traditional, a spot preserved for a faintly possible visit of royalty. The light filtered through the oil paper shogi which formed the sliding partitions. As decoration, there was one vase of flowers, and one scroll etched with a single white crane, and on the floor were six mats of golden-hued tatami.

Our hostess served tea, bringing in a brass basin filled with glowing charcoal, and over this on three prongs she placed a tea kettle. There was a tray of rice and raw fish, and we squatted to eat. We talked of California; carefully Cap got around to the reason our host had left there.

"Your exclusion act," he answered quietly, but his tone was such that I hastily admired the beauty of his garden.

A week or so later we came to Kobe, which seemed a part of Europe transported to the East. The electric train service is so excellent in Japan that white residents have homes in Kobe and businesses in Osaka. Cap located our automobile agency, and then found MacDonald, the manager, looking for us. He was excited at our arrival, for he had wondered about our delay, and he told us the publicity had been immense and was continuing, so he wanted to display the cars.

"We have fifteen mechanics loafing around the shop," said Mr. MacDonald, "waiting for a transfer to Osaka; I'll put every last one of them on your job. And you're not going to stay in a hotel. My wife's waiting for you; she'll have dinner ready — American food."

MacDonald took us to his home in a miniature English car and I doubt if any other make could have shot through the narrow, steep byways of Kobe. We were scarcely delayed when a student on a bicycle dashed from a hilly side lane, struck the car's hood and catapulted over it. The young man stood up, a bit dazed but unhurt; he bowed and apologized profoundly as he disentangled the smashed bicycle from our front fender. Mr. MacDonald appeared not to think the incident unusual, but we had no time to enquire into the ethics of Japanese car collisions.

Our hostess held out welcoming hands; servants knelt on the verandah to put cotton covers over our shoes. Here was another type of dwelling, half Japanese and Half American. The food was home-cooked, and I was not surprised when I found I was to sleep in a room decorated with pictures of Hiawatha, the "Vanishing American" and Buffalo Bill, while a Navajo blanket was spread over the spring-mattressed bed. It was in this house I had one of three baths which stand out as highlights among the events of that tour.

"Bath," I had demanded in Russian to a servant in the Vladivostok hotel when, equipped in my kimono, with towel, soap and sandals, I expected direction to a point down the corridor. I followed my guide; the chill and my flapping kimono made me realize I had been led to the hotel's main lobby. No one paid the slightest attention as I passed. I was sure I had said the correct Russian word for bath, but my guide was now taking me into the street and a biting north wind was cutting through my thin robe. We crossed to a large courtyard where the servant left me without a word. Then a woman attendant appeared in a doorway, smiled at my bewilderment and beckoned me through a door where great clouds of steam and a strong scent of lye soap reassured me I had not strayed. This was he public bathhouse.

But it was not until breakfast time in the MacDonald's Japanese home that I found I had deprived the family of their own nightly tub. The compliment of the first water had been paid to me. I pulled the rain plug from the square wooden tub filled with steaming water. I should have stood on the latticed flooring and dipped the water over myself — there was a dipper hanging in the cupboard-size bathroom. Instead I got into the water, quivering at its heat, and I had no ideas of dippers beyond what I had read about them as means for getting a drink in a farm-house kitchen.

It was in Kyoto that the maids led me to another steam-dimmed apartment when my tired muscles shrieked "bath" at me. I commenced scrubbing in the comparative privacy given by a three-foot partition. Filmed in a glaze of soap bubbles, I continued frothing them chin high when a masculine voice in well-accented English, complimented me on the film-lecture given the night before in one of the local theaters. My bathmate had been in the audience, and soap bubbles did not hide my identity.

Only one road leads from Kobe to Osaka. It was bordered by the slums of the nation, at least it appeared so to us on the morning we traveled over it. Its whole length seemed to be a cesspool of humanity, with filth and degradation around the outcasts of a race. The track was so narrow the cars barely edged through, and there were forty miles swarming with bullock carts, children, coolies with loads that dragged them down so that they walked almost doubled over, bicycle riders, women with kimonos open to the waist, plodding through the sloppy mud, and suckling grimy babies with eyes fly-tortured even in the cold. This was an appalling bit of Japan, but I had scarcely time to realize it when the squalor ended abruptly, fine gardens and parks came into view and well-dressed people took the place of the miserable groups we had passed.

We came now to a railroad track and, with Cap ahead as always, somehow my car stalled right on the rails. A siren warned shrilly, and I jumped out as a group of laborers came running and shouting. They had time to push the car over the level crossing, but as I helped I felt the wind suction of the electric express tear at my shirt back. I went limp against the side of the car.

"There's a limit to looking for thrills, Aloha!" That was Cap, with his voice hard and scornful, and I knew he had been frightened. He had come back when he heard the uproar of the natives. He hated to be given an unnecessary scare, but I could not help it. I had run out of gas.

The dapper little theater manager who had signed us up in Kobe for his Osaka theater, had a good sense for publicity. The Osaka hotel was mobbed with photographers and news reporters, and it was breathtaking to be the center of attraction like this again. A brass band hove into sight; the tune they played was "Marching through Georgia."

Cap collapsed with laughter. I did not get the joke until he told me: "I told the little guy I started this tour from Atlanta." Cap stammered between his gales of laughter, "Gosh, if there were a real Georgia man here, he'd shoot them!"

The band led a parade that stopped at the factory of every leading industrialist; there were handshakings, bowing and masses of chrysanthemums, real and paper ones, heaped upon me. I filled the car with them and felt like the queen of a carnival until we found ourselves in the Street of Forgetfulness, Dotombori, Osaka's cinema world. The whole avenue was lined with theaters. Our manager made a speech, the photographers' light bulbs flashed, the air was split with Banzais from the crowd.

This was great: If Tokyo equaled this welcome, we could afford to skip the Hawaiian detail, and get on to the Capetown-to-Cairo and the Great North Road. It fired my imagination, the story of it that I had read was great bit of writing; so Cap definitely decided that we would stay no longer in the States than to take time for renewal of car equipment at Detroit, where they were already expecting us, and we required new camera and film equipment. I was impatient to start.

"We can't do everything at once," said Cap. "We'll have to book the bigger cities across the States too. That African thing is going to be expensive and not much chance of earning."

Cap was right, of course, but I tore into the work at hand in Japan with new enthusiasm. I could not then, and cannot now, resist the lure of another continent.

A Crown Prince Bows

THE RIVAL theater in Tokyo hired a man to commit hara-kiri on the stage, as an attraction to compete for the crowds which clamored for admission to the place we were showing our films and giving the lectures. That the poor, deluded wretch, through unwise financial ventures had brought ruin and disgrace to his family and to retrieve his honor would have committed suicide anyhow, was not a great comfort to me, even if it was none of my business. Each day this protagonist rehearsed in person on the stage how he would commit the gory act. His gruesome exit from life was the last scene of the final evening's performance. The hara-kiri artist fell, stomach down, upon his sword. Our impresario reengaged "The Girl Who Drives Round the World" for a second week, and no one else had unfortunate financial ventures to oblige the opposition.

The Japanese showed genuine interest in our films and lectures. A surprising number understood English, but the chief cause of our unprecedented popularity was a fortuitous happening which came our way when we stopped in Kyoto. I had been shopping for kimonos, which I had to have made to measure, since I needed twice the length of goods as that used for Japanese sizes. I ordered tabi, or the soft shoes, and geta, high wooden outdoor cleats with straps to match the material.

In the hotel garden I found Cap with the cars lined up and the cameras set. I stared in surprise.

"The crown Prince of Japan is stopping on his way to the army maneuvers," Cap explained, and we waited. Late in the afternoon His Highness arrived, and we ground the cameras; the royal personage turned directly toward us, smiled, and bowed. The story reached Tokyo that we were royally recognized; the news ran like wildfire from village to village and city to city so that the populace was at our command.

Kyoto is the center of Japan's film industry, and we had the freedom of one studio for our film work. Here we met Onoe Matsunosuke, whom they described to us as the Errol Flynn of Japan. He and another actor staged a sword duel in costumes of the ancient Samurai, and I saw the Japanese idea of a "Western," in which no firearms were used, and no hero kissed the heroine even after desperate rescue.

It was not exciting.

The heavy rain turned to snow, and our way to Tokyo was complicated by meeting platoons of soldiers, with huge guns hauled by horses. They made boggier the tracks that served the section instead of roads. The horses reared and pawed the air in fright at the cars. There was mock warfare going on; if it had been real we should have been obliterated, since there was furious and deafening bombardment as we dragged behind the advancing troops. There was no way to pass them, and that's why when we came to a village we stayed at a Japanese inn.

The bowing proprietor, flanked by bowing servants, greeted us and apologized for living. We left off our shoes, the clerk sat upon his matting pouffe with the register across his knees, and as the maids came forward to show us our rooms, I caught a glimpse of Cap's big toe gaping beyond the sandal and out of his worn sock.

I followed my maid up a flight of stairs, steep and slippery and without banisters. A brass brazier heaped with hot charcoal stood in my room; I squatted awkwardly before it and the maid stared. I could not explain to her that I was terrified of splitting the knees of the only pair of English riding breeches I had left in my scanty outfit. The inn was clean and the food appetizing, so it was with good heart that we took the road in the morning.

We found that it forked off into a right and a left branch when we got well beyond the village. There was a significant Japanese mark on the signpost; if we compared our Japanese map and found a similar mark, then we had the right road. At the end of eighty minutes Cap gave in to my arguments, which I based upon a picture of Fujiyama, for we were bound for that mountain. We dodged small coverts of trees, stunted and wind-blown, swerved to avoid the barren yards of lonely farmhouses, and then we reached the frail weather-beaten timbers of a bridge across the swirling stream.

I drove straight for the dead center between the worn low railings, but as my front wheels hit the loose planks, the right front hub caught against a jutting post. I braked hard, and the recoil of the wheel as it freed itself flung the car against the next post. There was a crash, weak boards splintered and my car was over the side with flying timbers scattering round me. A stubborn railing stanchion caught the rear axles. It did not break and I found myself unhurt except for bruises, sitting right side up but suspended in midair, and Cap hauled me back to safety.

"We'll have to find help," he said as I regained my breath; "that post can't hold forever."

Still a bit dazed, I went in one direction and he in another, to hunt for brawn and muscle. We found peasants in the rice fields who were big, strong fellows. With long poles and superhuman effort, as it looked to me, those men set the car back on its four wheels.

Now the steep and dangerous road wound up from the rolling hills, and it became populated with white garbed pilgrims, a familiar sight to us in other parts of Japan. They plodded upward, leaning on long staffs. Cap stopped to warn me that the way was becoming steeper and still more dangerous, and that stop seemed a chance to photograph the pilgrims on the road to Fujiyama, one pilgrimage which is not entirely spiritual, but which the Japanese also look upon as one of physical readjustment.

"See if you can detain one of those women," said Cap, and I picked out a young mother with a jolly-looking baby strapped to her back. I bowed before her; the little person looked at me in surprise, then returned the bow so deeply that the baby looked straight into my face from over her head and gurgled with delight at this new sport. I kept bowing as Cap moved the camera round, and we got an amusing scene.

Japan honors these mountain devotees; officialdom places food in shrines for their use along the way, and even supplies cows stationed at intervals from which refreshment of milk may be taken if the cow is willing. Cap tried to induce an older pilgrim to take a lift in the car. He refused and an English-speaking student in the group explained that the old man was counting his steps from home to his first sight of the sacred mountain; since he had come over one hundred miles, his count must have been nearing the trillions.

There were ten miles of increasingly steep grade as we approached the minor mountain top from which Fujiyama is seen to greatest advantage. Cap came back on foot to help me negotiate the more ticklish spots, for the hairpin bends were becoming more frequent, and on the last six we could not drive; so with charming courtesy, pilgrims laid aside their straw matting bundles, their straw hats that eclipsed their heads to the shoulders, and the stout staves, to push the American cars around the turns. I was thankful we should not have to return the same way.

"Forward," I shouted, as I directed the car's progress, and all the directions were translated back to the pilgrims. It took us hours.

The summit was a grassy knoll beyond a pine forest, with the road ahead spiraling downward through the lesser peaks and disappearing into a valley which seemed to be a riot of color. Cap shut off his motor. I drew my car up beside his and then saw that he was standing silent and with his head bared as if he were in a cathedral. Fuji lay beyond. We watched until the sinking sun vanished and the white crest of the sacred mountain was bathed in a sea of carmine. Alien and travel-stained, I think I glimpsed there something of the soul that may once have breathed in old Japan.

Halfway down the mountain we came on the Fujiya Hotel, built in a great crescent, with magnificent gardens and a cascading waterfall, and we halted at Kamakura so that we could look at the colossal bronze Buddha which sits as it has for seven centuries, with worshiping throngs passing beneath it. This is the great Peace Buddha, cast from the molten weapons of the Samurai warriors when they united into one empire. It is a strange anomaly of civilization's march; once an earthquake moved the statue's base five feet, but the Peace Buddha stands unshaken, and Japan sweeps on with a trail of bombs marking her pathway.

Tokyo seemed to leap at us as we threaded the labyrinths of a pine forest near it. Our fame had preceded us; the story of the Crown Prince was on every tongue, and as we wound our way through the streets to the post office, first one car and then another joined in to follow us. We had a procession, with reporters, photographers and the merely curious. They followed me to the hotel but I refused to talk to anyone until I had opened at least one letter from my mother. It had been six months since we had had letters from home.

The Imperial Hotel at Tokyo is like a jewel plucked by a bold hand from some unborn epoch. Frank Lloyd Wright materialized an erratic dream, built half above and half below ground level, with swooping lines and low ceilings. I felt I had stepped into fairyland when I was within its corroded stone walls and under the flat eaves. I found my room was a symphony in all shades of blue, from a satin bedspread to a sky-blue ceiling.

Cap was doing penance over our Kyoto contract. Somehow he had let the Japanese manager get away with fifteen of our film-lectures for one hundred and fifty yen.

"Cap," I protested, "that's only fifty dollars."

"You talk with the next one yourself," said Cap, and with mighty self-confidence I set off to find the leading theatrical manager in Tokyo.

There was no trouble in making a contract. The manager sat at his desk, the top of it spread with headlined front pages of newspapers. I stood there, the flesh and blood counterpart of the full-length pictures of the heroine of the stories of the world-encircling stunt. I let the manager compare the printed pictures and me.

He spoke almost perfect English. "You want a theater?" he questioned.

"We're here for a week," I said, "then we sail for America. We'll spend two days advertising and five days showing the films; one thousand dollars American—take it or leave it." I nodded toward the window where outside the crowds were milling round my car, examining the complimentary plates of auto clubs from half the world. The sight of the crowd was convincing.

"All right," the manager said, "I'll get out posters. We'll do everything for you. You sign this contract please." The manager was wily; he knew perfectly well I was offering a real and new attraction for his theater; but the bargain was made, and certainly Tokyo made lions of us.

There was one sight in Tokyo someone dared me to see. It was the Yoshiwara, which I determined to visit.

There is a stern decree of Japanese life that the daughter of the house shall sacrifice everything to the family when need arises. That is why each new Japanese calamity of earthquake, tidal wave, near-famine, interior floods or whatnot, brings an influx of newcomers to Yoshiwara. Yet the population of Oirans, Queen of Flowers, Tokyo's public entertainers, does not fluctuate much within the Walled City as to numbers. That is why, too, many handreds of girls were reported to have been burned alive during a particularly violent earthquake. The city fathers held that the gates of Yoshiwara should remain locked, while the flames spread. They believed that death, bad as it might be for the victims, was better on the whole than flooding the country with the poor disfranchised blossoms who only know one profession.

There was a young Japanese graduate of an American university who offered to guide us amongst the Queen of Flowers. At the wooden gates he gave a password. Within, the village was symmetrically planned, and a pale yellowish light showed curved outlines of dwellings with elaborate entrances. We walked along the main thoroughfare to one of the brokers' offices of which there were several. In an open-fronted room a small Oriental squatted on a shelflike ledge. No difficulties were made for us. Ledgers were handed to us in which photographs of the girls were recorded with names, ages, weights and heights. There was a complete description of aptitudes a girl might have cultivated, and the subjects in which she was versed.

The broker was really helpful; he suggested we visit a young lady who spoke some English. The girl was amusing. Her frequent visitor was a young man from Chicago, and he taught her a specialized vocabulary which part of the time was pretty embarrassing. But the formality of our reception was as conventional at the White House, and our tour of the dwelling was quite circumspect. Several companions joined our hostess; they were gay, young and smiling and plucked the strings of their samisens, sang little ditties, drank tea, wandered off at a call to duty from the chief hostess. I took down the Japanese courtesy flags from the cars the next morning, and the Stars and Stripes waved alone.

Oh, Say Can You See!

I WAS not very old when my parents took me to Europe from the United States. I could remember things in a shadowy way, but no details, so our imminent arrival in San Francisco excited me; it was really like coming to another new country. I think I anticipated marvels. This "coming home" was to be one of the great experiences of my life. With such anticipations, it turned out differently. I tried to pierce the gloom of a murky fog hovering over the Golden Gate as a tug came out to meet our giant steamer. Reporters and cameramen who had come on the tug scattered over the ship seeking personages of importance. Somehow there was not the enthusiasm I had looked for.

"How many times was the car repaired? How many miles have you covered? How much would it have cost if someone financed the trip from the start? Momentarily my enthusiasm was dashed and my high hopes shattered. I tried to explain that money could not purchase the experiences we had had. The young man was not interested in that; he didn't care a hoot where we had been nor what we had seen, nor did he want impressions; he wanted facts.

It was cold and gloomy. At the Customs Office, Cap proudly produced the yellow clearance papers issued at the start of the round the world enterprise. I hated to give them up, for those pieces of paper had gone through many an international vicissitude. Often they had been dried out after a plunge through a river; they were mislaid once in India, and we thought they were lost. Cap had pulled them out of his leather pack often when the going was really hard, and said: "Never mind, these mean the United States."

The customs clerk was not at all interested; he spiked the papers on a pin file and asked:

"Now then, anything to declare?"

I suppose I expected a brass band and maybe a public reception; we had had them in many places. Everywhere the very sight of the cars had preluded interest. We seemed at the moment to be very much prophets in our own country.

I had never driven a car in America, and I guess Cap never thought of instructing me. He put his car into gear and set off for a hotel. There were streams of cars; I'd never seen so many, not even in London, and then I was not one of the drivers. They all moved in the same direction; they all stopped as though, trained, and every one stopped except me. I slammed into the car in front. A man jumped out asked me why the so-and-so-then he saw I was a girl, and asked for my license number. I pointed to the Japanese plate on my car.

"What the devil?"

The cars behind honed terrifyingly and the tempest of sound forced the man back to his own vehicle. Then there came a dreadful shrieking sound and the cars seemed to have gone mad, for magically a lane was made down the center of the street. Two motorcycles came through, and a red car with its siren screaming like a damned soul. I caught a glimpse of a corpulent officer smoking a cigar as he lolled back and his car split the traffic. I wondered what could have happened—certainly a major disaster.

Now I moved on as the cars moved and stopped with them. A bell rang ahead, and a mob of people dashed across the road before me. I saw a space wide enough for my car, and I edged in among the throng. Bedlam broke loose, angry pedestrians surrounded me, a policeman blew his whistle, then stepped from his island plot to accost me.

I planned quickly to follow the methods which had smoothed other situations nearly of this kind. As the policeman looked at the card he scratched his head, and I saw to my horror that he concluded I was foreign. Before I could explain he was waving his arms like a semaphore.

"Signal lights on the left side of the street," he said, speaking in a roaring voice—I knew that was to make the foreigner understand; I did it myself all the time when I did not know the language of a country. "Watch yourself; red means stop and green go." He cleared a space for me, but I am sure he thought I was an odd Jap.

Cap was waiting by the curb, and a great hotel loomed before us. The enormous lobby was brilliantly lighted; a squad of clerks were behind the desks and I had to giggle for I thought of the Japanese clerk with the register across his knee. Everywhere there were swirling and pushing people, so that I became dizzy; I think now there must have been a convention going on. But I discovered it was one thing to be the visiting white stranger among a lot of other nationals, and another thing to be a white stranger amongst one's own people.

"Wake up early," said Cap as I disappeared into the fastest elevator I'd ever been in.

The bell boy opened my door, put my bag and knapsack down and disappeared. I looked around and thought I must be back in Japan, for there was no bed. I opened the doors of closets and found a bathroom—such a glorious one! There was a cupboard for clothing; I found a bootrag and a bottle opener. I looked for a service bell, running my fingers carefully round the moldings of doors and windows. There was none. I opened the door and glanced along the corridor with a vista of endless doors all alike and all closed. No one came into view, so I returned to the room and spied a telephone on a recessed shelf. A crisp voice from the information desk explained where I would find a concealed lever which released the bed from the wall.

This was my own country. I tried to feel at home, and became steadily more mystified. We lunched in a cafeteria. The check for $1.75 for my overloaded tray gave me a first lesson on self-service restaurants. Cap laughed long and loudly, but he helped me eat the extra provisions, and paid for the whole thing; anyhow we'd had too many soy-bean meals to waste good foodstuffs.

"You'll learn," he said, "by trial and error."

Our next objective was Los Angeles. My heart sang with pride and joy at the grandeur and beauty of the California country as we drove along the lower coast highway.

Cap planned to leave me in Hollywood to do the laboratory work on our films, then he was to get another driver to take my car with his to Detroit for the promised overhaul, and that is how we found Owen, who came to Africa with us, then to South America, to Australia and New Zealand, and still is my faithful and zealous friend and aide.

The positive, vertical architecture of Los Angeles was something new to me also; the spirit of its plan, like fire and smoke that must soar to the skies, gave me a sense of elation. When I saw the Stars and Stripes flying high from some tall building, I really began to understand our acclaim for enterprise in other countries, because we had had that flag flying at the masthead of the cars no matter where we went. The streets seemed somber to me in all the sunshine, and they were hazy with gasoline fumes. I hired a car one day and drove out among the hills and orange groves. I met a tall boy wearing a sombrero and high-heeled, decorated boots, and I asked him where I could get something to eat.

"There's a cafe down aways," and he swung his arms vaguely toward the west. I drove five miles before I translated my own language to myself, but I found the café and ate hot cakes and syrup.

Before Cap and Owen left for the north there was a desultory interest shown in the cars when we parked them by the curb.

"That car is sure dolled up—all the bums come to Los Angeles in the season," I overheard, and burned with indignation. I know Cap pitied my mystification.

"What's your racket?" asked a man wearing a soiled overseas cap.

"My what?" I asked.

"Your racket—your gag?"

"Oh," I said, "just what you see on the car suggests a bit of exploration."

"Pretty well played out, ain't it?" spoke the knowing one from the side of his mouth.

"How's your racket?" I queried back.

"The soldier racket ain't what it used to be; used to rake off, don't know more."

Yet another man seemed interested in the number plates from many countries which were on one car.

"This car has just come across India, China, Siberia and Japan," I said as I pointed to the foreign license plates and club signs with which the cars were decorated.

The man looked at me and snorted:

"Yeh, I know—just another fake. There's a new one every day."

I drove on, for I was so disappointed. I had loved to talk with people before, because all of them seemed to have had some knowledge of the countries we had been in, and they liked to talk of the badges of those they knew. The sight of these trophies set them asking a thousand questions. I really felt sick at heart, but there was worse to befall me.

Cap had been gone two weeks; my studio work was coming along well, but more slowly than I had hoped for. The re-outfitting in Detroit for the Cape-to-Cairo trial was gaining momentum. I stopped on the steps of the post office to read my last letter from Cap and I smiled to myself, for he was so anxious to have the films and the cars ready together.

We proposed making a coast-to-coast tour of the States, the film-lectures earning the money in part for the South African enterprise.

"You're under arrest," said a voice at my elbow, and I looked up to see a man pulling aside the lapel of his coat where a bright badge shone, while he rolled a cigar from one side to the other of his mouth.

"But I haven't done anything. You must be making a mistake — why should I go to the police station with you?" The cigar took another rolling stance.

"If you know what's good for you, you're wearing United States Army equipment, impersonating an officer, that's what."

"Why," I almost laughed aloud in my relief, "I'm not a man, this isn't a uniform, it's not even the right color and my belt is Chinese. It's a pistol belt and the strap is over my left shoulder---"

"Tell it to the judge," he said.

There was a lot of delay but they asked for a $200 bond. I gave over the money. I wired Cap a long night letter, and found that I was really more confused than frightened. It did not occur to me to go to a lawyer because the whole thing seemed too ridiculous; that any officer would go out with shoulder length hair, wearing corduroy velvet jacket and breeches, was just absurd. This was the sort of fool things which happened in inner China or Manchuria, not America. Then when I saw the judge was a woman, I felt better — she was nice-looking, dark-eyed and buxom. I was convinced she would see the lunacy of accusing a girl of impersonating an army officer.

There were traffic violators, bootleggers, Mexican and Negro women of the streets in that crowded court room. I waited through a dozen cases.

"You are accused of infringing an army order regarding the use of the Sam Browne belt — guilty or not guilty?"

I was purple with indignation. "Not guilty, of course. This is a Chinese belt presented to me by a general in the

Chung Tso Lin forces at Mukden. An American officer's belt is smaller, lighter, and is work over the right shoulder."

The judge interrupted: "Are you or are you not wearing a leather strap over your shoulder?"

Of course I was wearing a belt; it was a Chinese souvenir and I was pretty proud of it. I valued it too for the way I had got it. The plain clothes man mumbled something for the judge to hear; I could catch nothing but "I've had enough—"

The judge cleared her throat: "Fined $200 or sixty days. Next case."

There was nothing to be done.

I had the money in my pocket, for Cap had left me plenty to take care of the film expenses. I paid the fine, and they gave me back the money I had posted. I figured that imprisonment in a mud hut among Chinese banditry was one thing; going to jail right in this place for something I had not done was not exactly my idea of adventure.

"Cap," I said, when he arrived by train a few days later "do you think we could finish the films somewhere else? I want to go somewhere where it is wild and fierce and uncivilized!"

"I'll stay down here until the films are done," said Cap, who did not worry half as much over the lost $200 as I did. It was Cap who made me feel a lot better when he found a cartoon in one of the papers showing the law caricatured as dragging a motorcycle policeman before the judge's bench.... "Your honor, I've just pinched a copy, was the caption. It seemed I had been the innocent victim of a feud long standing between Federal and State authorities, the Sam Browne belt being something coveted by the local policemen. There was nothing to be done about it.

"Another trial and error," said Cap, and he did not smile, so I do not know whether he meant to make the pun or not.

Revenge is not a part of my make up so the whole affair soon faded. I worked with fury on the films, cutting and assembling the pictures. Owen was already out booking the cross-continent tour, and there was a lot to be done. We needed more people for this tour, and a motorcycle in addition to the cars for an undertaking of this sort. There was good deal of interest at the automobile works in Detroit, and they were adding lots of convenient gadgets to the specially built cars. I wrote Mother at Nice and suggest that she and my sister Meg meet me in South Africa. I soon forgot my first experiences of my homeland in the applause, the newspaper eulogy and the success of our first appearances in the cities of the United States, and I made scores of friends.

Hark! The Hurricane

TWO WEEKS out from New York aboard the American-South African freighter Eastern Glade we sailed into one of those storms at sea which only can be described by a Conrad. I had a set of his works along; I bought the books when we put in at Norfolk to coal. There was a dense fog on that November day; the crash of coal going into the bunkers made me eager to be beyond hearing, so I went up into the city.

I came back to excitement; three German sailors had deserted ship and the skipper was raging. Cap, Smith and Owen volunteered for the jobs and were signed on for thirty dollars a piece to be paid at the end of the trip. The regular crew made no howl about union or that sort of thing when they found all three men had had sailing experience and held seamen's papers.

Smith was our new man, a short, lithe young English cockney, who answered our advertisement in New York for an interpreter, and who demonstrated he could speak half a dozen African native dialects fluently, and understand as many more. Our passports, visaed at the British Consular offices in New York, read like a page of romance: "Good for Union of South Africa, Rhodesia, Tanganyika, Uganda, Nigeria, Gold Coast and Sierra Leone." The cars were secured aboard, tuned to the nth degree with another overhauling at the factory. To our equipment we added a new movie camera. I had a new tropical outfit, and carried enough make up to last three months. I was proud to have designed a jacket useful for wear in jungle or on veldt, and in its pocket I carried a much read cablegram, for Mother and Meg had wired they would meet me in Johannesburg.

With Cap, Owen and Smith rated aboard as seamen, there were only three passengers left on the Eastern Glade. There was a middle-aged, gray-haired American nurse, wife of a missionary going out to join her husband in a God-forsaken part of the French Congo hinterland; there was a Rabbi going to a congregation in Capetown, and there was I.

The storm broke when we were fifteen days out from land bearing along the South Atlantic. The wind beat at us unmercifully. I tried to brace myself against the storm board which had been fastened to the side of my bunk so that I would not fall out. The walls of the cabin swayed and pitched, and when I tried to read I could not hold the book sufficiently steady to make out the jumbling type.

At daybreak I crawled up on deck, clinging to the storm lines strung its length, working cautiously toward the fo'c'sle, pausing now and then to catch my breath. It was November and almost a year to the day from our landing in Japan. I found Owen standing near the railing, looking utterly dejected. He waved me away.

"Don't come near me; two Germans in the crew are desperately ill, and it may be contagious."

"What is it? Who's taking care of them?" I shouted against the storm.

"It might be typhoid and there's no doctor. I've volunteered to nurse them."

"How about radio?" I called back.

"Try," Owen yelled and I went to the radio room. They picked up a vessel two hundred miles west, a French boat, and I translated the doctor's instructions for care of the men after our description of the symptoms were given. I wondered if the Captain's supplies contained the things needed.

There came a day of calm, gray weather, then dense fog and rising seas beat against our little ship with awful force. The wailing siren never ceased its banshee cry. The waves swept over the decks and frothed over the cars lashed and tarpaulin-covered. I feared they might be swept overboard and they were our stock-in-trade, barring the moving-picture films. We had added the motorcycle to the outfit, and much more in camping equipment comforts, and Cap had added a trailer to his car, which before long proved to have been a bad move. The wind shrieked in the rigging as we sank into the troughs of the mountainous waves, but the ship staggered on though every seam groaned.

Clinging to a stanchion, I yelled to Owen on the deck below: "How are the men?"

Owen clung to a rope; water soaked him to the waist as he swung on the pitch of a lurching roller. He looked drawn of face from loss of sleep, and haggard with his anxious responsibility.

"It's terrible," he said, "we have the old man under morphine—" and I could not hear the rest.

"Morphine, I said," Owen repeated, raising his voice and screaming against the tearing air. "He can't last but maybe we'll save the kid."

I was helpless standing there; all I could do was pull myself back to the cabin and there minister to the wife of the missionary, who was hardly conscious, being terribly ill with seasickness since the storm started. Through the porthole I could see swollen billows that looked solid as they came against us with a dull resounding thud. I dreaded the possibility of the cars being gone when I should reach deck again; I neither heard from Cap and Smith nor saw them. The sailor duties must have called for superhuman endurance, and the skipper never left the bridge. I saw the galley boy crawling up to him with gallon jugs of black coffee.

Sometime in the night I awoke to the realization of a strange quiet; the storm had blown itself out, or we had ridden through it. The ship was lifting over long, uneasy rolling swells of water, but the wind was down to a whisper. I got to the dining cabin on unsteady legs, just in time to overhear the first mate speak to the Rabbi, who went away with them. Then the cook brought in the meal and the Rabbi came back. He gulped down a cup of hot strong coffee, and his face showed gray-white above his neat black beard.

"Yes," he answered the question I had not put into words: "The sailor died at dawn; he has just had sea burial."

Then on a December day the first mate poked his head round the cabin door:

"Table Mountain in view," he said, and I led the meager passenger list up the companion way to the deck.

Table Mountain loomed black and majestic, a horizontal cut two miles across the sky, and along the crest white clouds spread like the table cover in a giant's home. The ship's engineers were idling; we swung about with the tide and were alongside the dock in Capetown. I was at a more mysterious end of Africa, and the sun was rising over white homes and the corrugated roofs of the dockside sheds.

We ran into trouble first thing. Although Pretoria, the capital city of South Africa, was eleven hundred miles away, the Capetown officials refused entry of our cars until permission came from the capital. That was a blow; we had not figured on two weeks' delay in Capetown, nor had we figured on laughter at our enterprise. Reporters interviewed us and howled.

"Cape to Cairo over the Great North Road," I announced complacently.

"There is no road," came the reply that flabbergasted me.

"I read an article in the American papers," I said. "What about the Court Treatt expedition — ?"

I trailed off my sentence into a question mark and learned that a man had pioneered the trail in 1924, reached Southern Rhodesia and was mauled to death by a leopard;

the Court Treatt expedition made a valiant attempt, and took eighteen months on the road. Eight months were spent in preparation, with an investment of many thousands of dollars, and even dumps of spare parts, tires, fuel, food and sacks of small coins, were made along the way before the actual start. But nothing broke our spirit. We added a useful slogan to our daily conversation: "Where there's a trail there is a way," and it was an inspiration which helped us through hard days to come.

On the day permission came to clear the cars, I wired Meg in Johannesburg: "Pack your bag, join us here, leaving for Cairo Monday;" and Meg replied: "Meet Kaffir Mail."

My sister Meg was a pathetic-looking young lady, gray with dust after her five days on the train, but her spirits were high when I bade her hop on the motorcycle behind me and we made for the hotel.

"You'd better get used to the bike," I told her, "for you and Cap will lead the procession when we leave on our great trek."

Nothing was likely to daunt my sister.

That is exactly how we traveled, Cap and Meg breaking trail, Owen driving with Smith in Cap's old car and the new trailer added to it to carry spare gas, and I drove my own old car.

At Port Elizabeth, several weeks later, we added Felix Vanloon to the crew. He was a seventeen-year-old Boer from up country who was to prove invaluable to the outfit in his knowledge of northern tribes and the kitchen Kaffir dialect used between whites and natives of the Union as a means of communication. We horrified officials and newsmen by announcing that we would take no native boys along. They told us that idea was a breach of etiquette in the first place, and foolhardy in the second. We could not afford boys. Like it or not, the tasks considered menial had to be done for ourselves by ourselves. We had embarked upon the crossing of four thousand miles of mystery, and our preparations, as I look back on them now, were sketchy and meager.

By a warm Christmas Day we were headed well on the way for up-country.

The Verdompt Thing

THE PROPHETS of misery among officials and newspaper men had been busy. I looked for untoward events day by day, and maybe that anticipation started the chain unwinding, but it was five days from our start on the road when the first disaster met and overtook us. We had reached a mountain pass before Oudtshoorn, and as my car reached the summit I found the motorcycle in a ditch, Cap and Meg nursing knees and elbows that were raw, with sand embedded in the cuts. Neither could tell what had happened; they found themselves in the ditch, that was all, and fortunately the engine of their vehicle ceased firing. Our first-aid kit was in Owen's car, which stuck at the foot of the hill, so that, minus two helpers, we spent a full day pushing and hauling her up. That is when the name of "verdompt thing" was given our new trailer acquisition.

We were going over veldt now, gray and without vegetation, except for the kloofs, or valleys. To keep three vehicles on the same trail was a heavy task. Someone was always coming to grief, or getting lost.

At east London we figured out a method of mapping directions for ourselves. We were now heading inland to Cloemfontein, and search as we might, no detailed route map materialized. We consulted garage men, then conferred together combined the salient points, and a master map with detail was drafted for each driver. The most frequent of these direction sheets read something like this:

"As you reach outskirts of city, Uitenhage, follow right of railroad for five miles, cross tracks, keep left across country; at first *kopje* turn right, at fourth gate take left branch trail; when railroad is struck again, take best trail."

We calculated a certain amount of tentative mileage to be covered each day, which might brings us to a suitable camping place to be chosen by the motorcyclists and trail breakers.

We moved now over territory marked by sheep barriers, a mile separating one boundary of a ranch from the other. At each line barbed-wire fences and long iron gates carried the legend:

"Maak to die Heck and use Cooper's dip." It amused us at first, then irritated us.

In twenty miles we opened and closed twenty gates; the fine was two hundred and fifty dollars if we did not close them. We had no sheep and therefore no use for Cooper's dip. The days became hotter, the nights colder, the country opened up into rolling miles of brown-gray veldt, spotted with groves of cacti. At night we camped, Meg and I sleeping in my car and the men in tents. Beyond the *dorps*, villages or towns where we had been purchasing food, there was always dust and scrubby grass, and soon the *dorps* ceased to appear, and we depended on what game we could find for our main fare.

The trailer was a dire mistake. It was too heavy and was eternally becoming stuck and always delaying us. We determined to trade this in Johannesburg; the resulting bargain gave us a light vehicle capable of remodeling into the touring, low-slung pattern that suited us best. Travel seemed a little easier.

But we were still a long trek from Jo'burg. Fresh meat was needed. Cap and Meg started across the veldt on the motorcycle, blushed a herd of springbok, the graceful deer whose image is on the coat of arms of the South African Union. Meg reached for the Parabellum, Cap rested the muzzle on his arm as he brought the cycle to a stand. He aimed, fired, and one animal leaped high in the air and fell while the others stampeded. Cap raced the cycle toward the wounded 'bok. It raised its head, looked at him with pitiful liquid brown eyes, human in their pleading and Cap put it out of its pain. Then he lowered the gun and said: "I shall never kill anything again as long as I live," and he meant that.

They strapped the springbok on the back of the bike, then drove on to reach the point of rendezvous arranged for the night. But that was not the end. The Boer, owner of the ranch, had heard the shots. His powerful car overhauled the cyclists.

Cap was startled at sound of a voice:

"You have shot a springbok on private property; the hunting season is over, I must report you, and now you will come with me."

Already feeling badly, Cap made no protest, but followed the big Boer beyond a knoll behind which was a corral of long-horned cattle. Further on were barns, then the trail turned on to a well-beaten track through mealier fields and to a shed. From this parking place, the culprits went to a low-eaved thatch-roofed house, with white pillars supporting the shady front *stoep*. Inside it was a typical *voortrekkers'* home. Leopard skins covered the earth-packed floors; on one whitewashed wall was a picture of Oom Paul Kruger, one-time president of the Boer Republic; on another was that of General de Vedt, uncle of the ranch owner. At the door of the room rested a stack of rifles, and on the mantel shelf of an open fireplace was the polished skull of a leopard, with huge teeth gleaming, and wide antlers hung over the doorway. It was here that Meg and Cap first heard a leopard called a tiger, which is common in South Africa, although there are no tigers in the country.

A native answered the handclap of the Boer, who gave an order in Afrikaans. The man's wife, a plain-faced daughter, two husky and surly-looking sons came in and seated themselves round a plain board table. The Boer at the top of this arraigned his prisoners. Speech was a difficulty until Cap used a couple of German phrases to illustrate a point, and thus discovered that the Boer spoke fluent German. Thus the misunderstanding was cleared up and Cap was presented with the springbok meat, as he explained our enterprise, which intrigued the Boer family. Even the surly faces of the silent sons lightened somewhat as they heard of China, India and Siberia. The mysterious shadows of an African night were overcasting the gorgeous greens and scarlets of sunset when Meg and Cap overtook us as we outspanned for another rest.

Africa looked as though it were going to become a long monotonous chain, links of *dorps* punctuated by larger cities, all strung across uncounted miles of dusty gray-brown *veldt*. We rose at dawn, outspanned at sunset, and I wrote my diary by the light of a camp fire, and I tried to soak myself in the extraordinary "feel" of this strangest of continents. It is a vast place and of infinite variety.

News at Bloemfontein changed the scene for us. There was report of a new diamond field discovery at Lichtenburg, Transvaal. In the midst of one of our lectures, the Bloemfontein theater emptied as though for a fire alarm. Someone had passed in the word of a diamond rush, and the date of the ground release.

"Let us go," I said to Cap as we stopped the projector running and looked at the empty seats.

"Sure, let us go," echoed Cap. The next day we pulled stakes and joined the rush northward.

We reached Lichtenburg on the evening before the opening day, and I watched a line of prospectors stretched across the flat open plain, five thousand men, white, black and yellow, the line held back by mounted police, although there seemed no inclination to break it or take an unfair advantage. Each man was grasping a small wooden peg with which to stake his claim on the world's greatest diamond bed. I saw husky black native runners in the crowd, pioneer Boers in tattered felt terrain and homemade veldtschoen. I saw young bloods from Rhodesia, and rosy-faced lithe lads freshly out from England. I could have guessed their homes as being in some ivy-clad rectory.

Thousands of trek wagons lumbered through the churned earth, loaded with supplies, and oxen groaning as they hauled. In four days there had risen a public kitchen place; a printing press was in operation. There was electricity, and we, the people of a crazy world tour, were "turning 'em away" at the Diggers' Biograph.

Our show lasted four nights; on the fifth someone started a gun fight, and our hired projectionist became a corpse. He had been a local man we picked up, but this was a community of primitive men, with all the instincts of passion, greed and inhumanity to their fellow man right there in the raw. I watched over Meg like a clucking hen. Without an operator there was no show. We had been dipping rather heavily into the exchequer. Meg had her uke, I had my trusty guitar with which I had replaced the samisen I had left in the States, Owen and Van proved keen musicians, and Cap was no mean pianist—there was a piano in the Bio. An idea struck me which seemed pretty good:

"Suppose we start a dance club, Cap?"

Cap was not in favor of the scheme, but we really had to earn something for expenses in Jo'burg and beyond so we packed the valuable films with care and turned the theater into a dancing place, and ourselves into a jazz orchestra of sorts. It served. In the day time we, Meg and I, dug and delved for small diamonds, but outside Jo'burg we lost all we had garnered. We were outspanned in a lovely willow grove by the Vaal River, so Meg and I dumped our shirts in the stream to rid them of accumulated travel stains. We forgot about the diamonds secreted in the breast pockets, and washed a very modest fortune away in an excess of cleanliness.

Mother, as unofficial publicity agent in Johannesburg, had been worth her weight in diamonds. A brass band met us at the outskirts, newsmen mobbed us, and photographers begged us to look pleasant, while we rode to the city hall and were received by the Mayor. It was a great occasion. The minor difficulties of getting new permits for our meager equipment of firearms cast barely a shadow of annoyance. There were gay moments and also sad, for mother left us then for a tropical haven in the West Indies.

Now Cap went alone on the motorcycle, leading us northwest into the mountainous country toward Lydenburg. Meg and I, with Van, Owen and Smith, followed in the two cars, I sticking stubbornly to the wheel every mile of the way, for ambition to drive to Cairo had not lessened.

Near Lydenburg are the famous platinum mines of the Northern Transvaal. We lingered at an East Indian trading post, picturesque under the shade of a giant Boab tree, and we watched a group of Mavenda girls come to trade. It was the monthly pay-day spree of these tall, lithe, beautifully proportioned young women. Their costumes were unique, and I wanted to photograph the girls who were picturesquely garbed, to our surprise, in finely tailored calico garments, bought from the astute Goanese barterer. The costume's bright bodice had tight, short sleeves; a full frill from neck down half covered the breast, and a nude space ended at the hips from which a gaudy frilled skirt sagged with the weight of many rows of white beads. Dozens of anklets made of bright yellow wood made a dull, melodious thunk, thunk as the girls walked. I had to call Meg with a second camera to photograph me photographing the native women, for as I bent to look in my camera, they clamored round and wanted to see into the finder also. Each girl carried a long staff flying a white paper ribbon, as presently they sauntered off, taking with them the trinkets they had bought—all there was to show for their husbands' wages. They chattered like monkeys.

"Let's follow them, Cap," I begged, and we ran on a trail at the base of a kopje. We passed the girls and then sought for the branch track to the north, with the car wheels plowing deep into fly-sand. An hour later, rounding a bend we met the girls again. We had completed a circle of the *kopje* and missed the trail.

Darkness came as we crossed the Olefantes Valley, the bed of it a wreckage of potholes, long cracks in the dried mud and boulders displaced by the last seasonal torrent. The Goanese trader warned us not to stop here too long. We dared not outspan lest the rain come and the torrent sweep down, which would mean we would be held there for days. We set our path by the queer glow of an unexpected light hanging low in the sky, and above the roar of the struggling motors came the beat of tom-toms. We left the cars and advanced cautiously until we could see black shadows that danced across the lurid light.

The magnet of wood and warmth drew us closer, then we stopped short of the circle of firelight and peered at a fantastically accoutered group of natives. They wailed, they yelled; grotesque figures leaped, threw themselves into tortured shapes that bordered on obscenities. We drew back to the cars. Two women, stark naked reeling under the mad headiness of Kaffir beer, reached the cars. We had encountered no hostile natives before so when the women spat on the car and began to scream insanely, we sprang to the wheels and backed off to the distant river bank

Before midnight a swift stream of water barred our path and we halted. Our headlights glowed on a small patch of rushing water, and from downstream came the muffled roar of falls. This was the Olefantes ford.

"Dark waters usually mean crocodiles," said Smith.

"Drunken natives usually mean murders," said Van.

"We've a couple of young women with us," Young Van spoke again, and added: "I've done this sort of thing before; I'll wade across and see how the bottom goes."

"Shall we let him, Aloha?" More and more frequently now decisions such as this were being left to me. That Cap was training me to leadership I know now, but I did not realize it then. I might be sending a man to his death; he was old in experiences such as this, but a lad in years. There were Kaffirs behind us, wild with liquor, and I was responsible for Meg. I had seen the viciousness of Chinese bandits toward their own kind, and now we were in Africa, minus any kind of civilization as far as this type of native was concerned, so what might not they do upon white people?

"Go ahead, Van," I said aloud; then, tense, waiting, praying as he stepped into the water I stood with Meg clutching my hand. We strained our eyes in the faint path of white thrown by our headlights and on to the dark void beyond into which the boy disappeared; the roar of the cataract seemed to be closer than before, and the echo of those tom-toms was in my ears.

Then, silence, but for the lapping surge of water. Presently came a shout, and we strained our ears to make out words.

"The water is shallow, deepest spot up to my knees and about fifty yards wide; keep a straight line from where you are, there's a high ridge at the crossing. Up and down stream the bed falls away into deep water; come straight as you can to the sound of my voice."

I started my engine, and plunged the car into the stream first. Meg was with me. Cap, Smith and Owen stayed by the second car, and hoisted the motorcycle to the low baggage-board. Two of them strained to hold it, and Smith drove.

"Ho—ho—a—ho!" Van's voice, young and clear, became more distinct. I steered by the sound; the water lapped to the hubs, spurts of it swished round our feet, and I prayed that the engine would not stall. There came a sharp rise under us and I put my foot down heavy on the gas to urge the flivver on. We had reached the other bank. I turned and my headlights threw a beam for the second car.

Overhead were the spreading branches of a Boab tree, so, weary to exhaustion, the men gathered thornbush for the watch fires, and we placed the cars in pioneer laager formation. It is a variation of the old covered wagon train encampment, used when our forefathers crossed the American prairie, and developed by the Boer trekker.

I awoke as dawn streaked the sky and I roused Meg so that we might slip down to the river to bathe. A hundred yards below the fording place of the night before, almost lost in a swirl of foam and mist, we found the cataract that swept over the ledge into a whirlpool below. It was beautiful. Further up we found a quiet backwater where glistening brown water shone under green foliage, and we could see the clean sandy bottom. Silver blades of light shone on the horizon beyond purple-blue *kopjes*, the birds were twittering, insects scattered as we disturbed them in the light underbrush. Meg and I frolicked in water that proved pure as crystal and cold as ice.

A few miles from the Olefantes River we drew into a *dorp* where we patched and repaired our thorn-scratched bodies, our clothing and our cars. Our next objective was through Louis Trechard to Messina, a copper mining area on the great Limpopo river, the natural boundary between Rhodesia, the Transvaal and Portuguese East Africa.

At Messina, two water towers marked an end of the South African railway system. Here was a small group of European-type houses, with scraggly gardens cowering away from the native kraal. We saw mine shafts bordering the town; in front of the hotel, trek wagons stood laden with sacks, and long spans of tired little donkeys stood dispiritedly under guardianship of native boys who lay indolent and asleep on the wagon tops.

"There are two Englishmen here," said Smith suddenly. We looked at him in amazement, for there was not a soul in sight but the sleeping natives.

"Have you been here before?" I asked him.

"No," said Smith; and in the same breath, "There, you see," and he pointed to an arid square of beaten-down earth near the depot, "there is a tennis court."

It was; and there were two Englishmen in the dismal hole. There was a bridge, too, of saplings and mud stretched from bank to bank of the Limpopo. We could see the British flag waving over a government boma, or courthouse; as we came near it, two Askaris in khaki shorts and red fezzes stood to attention.

It had taken us exactly five months to the day to reach the Rhodesian border from Capetown.

King of Pafuri

"I'LL TAKE your word of honor you will not try to steal across the border," were the last doleful words I heard the young official say, for I went out of the boma and sat down on a log outside and practically howled.

We'd been refused permission to travel through Southern Rhodesia. Why? Nobody knew, least of all the distressed young man who had to turn us back.

We made camp on the Transvaal bank of the Limpopo River, and after dusk Owen bagged a hare, of which Van made a stew. The rest of us built a six-foot corral of thornbush round our bivouac. That was protection against man-eaters; the young chief at the boma had told us there were plenty about. He was really concerned about us, but he had to obey orders.

"Let's sing," I said to the others; but if the music held our nerves in check, it did not solve our problems.

"Suppose we wire the government at Salisbury," was Cap's suggestion.

That wire had one hundred and thirty words in it. We promised merely to cross Southern Rhodesia in a straight run, pausing only for food, sleep and repairs—we would not take photographs if they did not want us to, and we would not show the films we had of other countries, nor try to book theater appearances.

"Three days before you can look for a reply," said the telegraph operator at Messina. Three days, and Salisbury was only three hundred and fifty miles away! Well, it might be for the best, we concluded, and we needed a rest. We moved to a more habitable camp and prepared to take things easy, our minds filled with hope.

The reply to our telegram came in five days, and it was a polite but uncompromising "No!" We canvassed every possibility as to the reason for refusal. Our passports visaed in New York, stated, "Good for Rhodesia," in addition to other parts of the country. It was not until I was on my third African tour that I found out the real reason. That "Soviet Colonel" title of mine, and our Mukden, Siberia, Harbin, Vladivostok and Soviet army pictures, shown in all openness and good faith, had given us a fatal brand—communist propagandists. Why it did not worry any other part of the country, but only Southern Rhodesia, is still a mystery.

The Governor's compliments accompanied his profound regrets at loss of our transient company, but I was so angry and disappointed that I went off by myself then returned to camp quickly for the maps we had, because a thought had come to me.

"Come here, Cap," I said, "Can't we detour this Rhodesia? I bet there's a way through Mozambique—Portuguese East, you know."

No one of the party commented, for no one knew, but an hour or so later when we stood outside the terminal the African railroad, I watched a span of sixteen donkeys drawing to a stop to park a dusty, covered trek wagon at the hotel across the road. Fate marched by that wagon in the person of an ancient Boer, weatherbeaten of feature and seasoned in his style. He laid aside his rawhide *sjambok* as I went over to him, and performed the necessary courtesy of getting rid of his tobacco stream.

"Do you know if there's a trail north by way of Portuguese East?" I asked.

The old Boer ruminated and I tried to make the question clearer, but he understood English quite well.

"We want to follow the Limpopo to its junction with the Pafuri, I think, then cut north and cross the Sabi—can it be done with automobiles?"

The old chap removed his hat, scratched his head and thought he recalled a trek into Portuguese bush thirty years back; but he was quite sure about one thing, now an Englishman called Stetson lived near the border.

"Take the route back to Louis Trechard," said the Boer, who was becoming interested; "Get your provisions and gasoline there. You ought to swing northeast along the Limpopo, and make the river junction. If Stetson, the Englishman, is still there, he'll put you right on the next lap."

We were profoundly grateful; this was the first definite information concerning the territory that we had had and we put about to Louis Trechard without delay. There was a deluge of rain sweeping that *dorp* like a torrent as we drove in. Cap hustled Meg and me to a lodging house and told us the boys and he would camp in the blacksmith's yard.

"The minimum of equipment," ordered Cap, and had everything brought to our rooms so that with Meg's aid I could sort the things down to the limit of need. Shorts, shirt, hat, shoes and one blanket apiece made up the wardrobe. We laid in iron rations for a stiff trek. There was a fifty-pound sack of mealie-meal, twenty-five pounds of dried fruit and a hundred pounds of dried peas, with three tins of cocoa, four large cans of milk, five pounds of sugar and twenty pounds of salt by way of luxuries. We had trading stuff, too: rock salt, small coins in sacks—the coins called tiki—beads and safety pins. The men paid twenty-seven shillings a case, or eighty cents a gallon, for gasoline and bought all there was money for. We carried oil too, for we had no idea how long we might be on the trail, and Cap traded in the motorcycle on our supplies, taking a real loss on it.

"You are utterly mad to attempt it," said everyone living in Louis Trechard as each person took opportunity to stop us and speak.

"Your supplies will not last; you won't have enough fuel."

"Everyone tells us what we won't have," I said to the Louis Trechard doctor on the last day of our stay there. "Doesn't anyone know what we will have?"

"I Do," said he, "but I hate to tell you. There's constant danger of malaria; you may find rains failing, which means thirst; and it's the richest lion and tiger [leopard] country known. Besides some of the natives are none too pleasant— it's not British territory you know, and the government of the native is on a different method—that is, after you leave Pafuri."

That did give me pause, and I got another jolt the same day as two large trucks pulled into the *dorp*, drawn by oxen. One carried the colossal head of a great bull elephant, the other had the feet and hide. They came from the direction of preserve country, where shooting merits a heavy fine. If they were poachers, they had a good story ready, telling us they had stampeded a herd near the Portuguese border and that the monster was for the Field Museum in Chicago. I went to the Museum afterward to see if I could find that head, and I never did.

"Darkest Africa, my friends," said Cap, as we set out that day. I felt a bit strange, too; this deliberate getting out of contact with white men might not be so wise. We followed the trail of a wagon until the afternoon, when we caught our first glimpse of the fringe of *bushveldt*. It was like a curtain of flat-topped trees coming toward us, the branches of thin foliage meeting overhead. We pulled up to watch our first herd of waterbuck, with gracefully twisted antlers, and their donkey-headed females. In the bed of a stream we surprised a pair of kudu which, when they scented us, held arched necks high, then dashed away with the speed of a bullet. We topped a hill an hour before dusk, and saw Cap standing on the summit beside his car.

"Lions," he shouted; "I just saw one bound away."

The trail became worse, the cars plowing along sand ruts, and through the gathering gloom ahead I was relieved to see the flicker of a camp fire. This was a Boer outspan. A man leaned against the high wheel of the wagon. The pungent aroma of coffee came on the air, the delicious smell of meat and oil dumplings, and with one accord we all knew we were famished.

The *voortrekker* gave us right hearty greeting, but did not cease the cleaning of his rifle; his wife, smiling and kindly, went on with meal preparation; somewhere beyond the firelight wagon boys beat a tom-tom. I could hear an elusive low soft tinkling and found that it came from a sort of marimba one of them played.

This *voortrekker* knew the country blindfolded; he was a mine of information, and we kept him up late finding out about the terrain.

It was nearly noon, two days later, when the trail took an upturn with a grade the cars could barely make; we took a breather on the brow of the hill, and saw a khaki-clad figure approaching us. We could guess his nationality even without knowing there was only one white man in the district. It was Stetson.

"By Jove, what are you doing here?" he shouted, and commenced running toward us. His clothes alone would have spotted him. He had creases in his shorts, his mosquito boots were polished and he smoked a pipe that could have originated only in one place.

"Hoping to get through to the Sabi River," I replied, before we explained who we were.

"Rather a sizable task. Come, get out of the cars—come on in, you must spend a few nights here."

Smith's sharp nose twitched as Stetson replaced his pipe in his mouth and the fragrance of his tobacco reached us.

"My name's Smith, England is my home, down Stepney way. I'll trade you two cigarettes for enough tobacco to fill my briar."

Stetson smiled. Smith was pure Cockney, and he prefaced every opinion with the ridiculous phrase "I myself personally." I saw that Stetson was chuckling to himself as he led the way to the central building of the boma.

"I'll accept the fags later," he said, "and you can have all the tobacco you want. They supply me regularly."

Stetson looked like Clark Gable; he was tall and pleasant spoken. Two beautiful greyhounds rushed to him for attention as he led the way to the station, which was set on the highest elevation in sight. In the rear, under shade of high trees, I could see a workshop, a kitchen kia, storehouse and a trading post. The *kopje* was thickly wooded so the whitewashed house with its thick thatched roof and low overhanging eaves was cool. Along these eaves little gray monkeys chased each other and chattered. I thought of Chango, and told Stetson about him; he quite believed that my monkey had been able to recognize certain scenes in the moving pictures.

This last outpost of empire had the flag flying; on a second *kopje*, across a deep ravine, were a group of thatched rondavels, beyond that a cattle stockade, and still further was where the native boys lived. I gazed utterly fascinated by the panorama of the Pafuri valley, the river losing itself in matted jungle, and the country beyond rearing for miles as on a relief map. It was my first sight of real African jungle. Privately I thought it must be impassable to man afoot, much less to two cars with six travelers.

"A bit of orl right, orl right, I myself personally think," said Smith, as we reached our host's sitting room, luxurious with bookshelves, tables, easy chairs, a grand fireplace and neatly piled racks of outdated newspapers.

"You're really not strangers to me," said our host as he pointed to all the papers. "I've seen the headlines about you—I'm really counting on your staying here a week or two; I want to hear about this globe tour at first hand."

"We'll run off a show of films for you," I volunteered, and then remembered the lack of electricity, so we could only show the stills.

Dinner was of roast chicken, which I was enjoying tremendously when a bonne bouche of white meat on my plate was suddenly snatched from beneath my eyes. I gave chase, but the audacious monkey, adventuring through the screen door which had not been latched, had made good his escape and I could not reach him. I returned to the table breathless, to take part in the discussion with Stetson on life at the edge of the jungle as the central theme.

"Fair play is the success secret of dealing with natives," he said. "That, and like children they must be able to trust you, yet they must also be made to feel a firm guiding hand. They call me 'M'Noti,' meaning 'he who whistles.'"

We could understand that, for Stetson was of frank manners and had a boyish laugh. He used it cheerily when he told how a London firm kept him in touch with civilization with records, books and magazines brought in by the trek wagon every six weeks, and he had six months' leave to look forward to at the end of three years. The radio reception so far had proved more or less of a failure, and that had been a disappointment, but it was his entire lack of white companionship that puzzled me.

"Why don't you have a wife?" I asked bluntly.

"Good idea," said Stetson, "but one girl in ten thousand reared in civilization could stand this place for long, and I've never met the ten thousandth."

But the important thing to us was that Stetson could tell us of the route we proposed to follow. We told him of the Rhodesian governor's refusal of transit permit.

"Incomprehensible," he said, and then added: "Frankly, I advise you to give up this idea. I know you want the film pictures, and that you want to be first to make the drive, but there is the merest trail from here to Chi Cuala-Cuala, and that is forty miles. I doubt whether the old Portuguese Commandant will give you leave to enter the Mozambique territory too far. He keeps people out on principle. I'd suggest getting down to a port, ship north and travel by car where it is more practicable."

But that was getting away from our idea.

"You see," explained Cap, "Aloha has been the first and youngest driver in these other countries. It would be—"

I interrupted him. "Just impossible to turn back now; we just must go."

"I'll question the runner I use between here and the Commandant; I have to consult him about my boys occasionally, besides you'll need his permit. Meanwhile, make yourselves at home here.

The days that followed were glorious. Meg and I haunted the native kraal, to find that the most amazing thing to the native women was the difference in our voices. Where our tones in speaking were soprano, the native women's could be classed as bass. They imitated my laugh and gestures, and were especially interested in my long fair hair, since their hair is black, kinked and makes a real mat on the head. They would not trust their children with us for some time, and neither Meg nor I was ever safe from window-peepers of our own sex. They could not quite grasp the whiteness of our skin where the sun had not bronzed us, and the mystery of our wearing clothing all over our persons was never solved. We even put on covering when we swam in the pool!

The staple native food was mealie-meal, or the local grown cracked corn. At times the women ground the kernels into meal and stirred it into a porridge in the typical three-legged Kaffir pot, one of which we carried in our own equipment. They ate meat cut into strips and dried in the sun to be eaten hard, the colloquial name of *biltong* being given it. When later we were overtaken by drought, and, passing many deserted villages, found ourselves mighty short of food, we learned that corn and biltong are a most sustaining diet. We used rock salt for trade as we advanced further and further from civilization, trading half a pound of it for ten pounds of maize.

Down the steep bluffs, the road plunges from the Stetson station into the depths of the jungle in the Pafuri valley. We explored within what Stetson called the safety zone. A sudden gloom always overtook us as we left the open trail, and we noted the rich contrasting greens in the vegetation which made a sort of magnificent twilight. Above our heads the foliage overlapped and entwined so that no ray of the tropical sun penetrated. There was wild confusion of branches, vines creepers, flowers and leaves. Underneath our feet was jet black loam and a carpet of empty pods from the giant bean tree which made a crisp staccato with each step we took; the colored seeds were strewn like a mad red hail which never melted. I saw giant-sized cabbage lichens, and all around was a curious but definite sense of struggle — life and death — dank earth, rotting vegetation. A hundred and fifty feet above us we could see baboons swinging from limb to limb. It was all thrilling and frightening by turns. Three miles of going through this verdure and we came on a two-acre clearing. This was Stetson's truck garden. We pulled oranges, tangerines and papayas, and left the black boys to haul back the prosaic carrots, potatoes, beets and cabbages; we really might have been in the backyard of any home of a thrifty American small-town householder, if we shut our eyes to the jungle, and if we had lost our sense of smell.

From this garden we caught our first sight of the Pafuri. It was a dark brown stream, glinting like bronze in sunshine. It has a sluggish current, but the river makes a complete break in the forest, for no trees at this point entangle above it.

Stetson spoke into the silence, as we stood and looked at the river below. "How would you like to experience a crocodile hunt?"

And the King of Beasts

THE RUNNER from Chi Cuala-Cuala arrived on the evening we killed—and photographed—two crocodiles on the banks of the Pafuri River. The runner spoke a jargon even Stetson could not understand, neither could Smith or Van. A native from the kitchen kia took the long-limbed stalwart black aside, clad in his full dress outfit of a buckskin apron, and questioned him. Then we discovered there was a note clipped in the top end of his long staff. This was a communiqué from Mongoni, Commandant at Chi Cuala-Cuala, his name, as we found out later, entirely appropriate as it was given him by the blacks. Mongoni translates into "He who cheats the natives."

In reply to Stetson's questions, the runner swung his arm from one horizon to the other, twice, following the arc of the sun. This meant it had been a two days' trip for a runner. The communiqué informed Stetson that his friends might cross the territory under Mongoni's control; that was as far as Sabi. From the incoherent explanations of the black and the interpreter, we gathered we could look for about five miles of dried river bed and sandbanks, with stretches of bush and water between. The only deep stream to cross was a twisting bend of the Limpopo, and through there a span of oxen could easily tow *lo stutu*, otherwise the cars, or thundermakers.

The interest in our coming trip was broken when the rejoicings started over the black boys hauling up the crocodiles taken in the hunt. Stetson had arranged it perfectly for us, first ordering a motorboat from his boathouse, another convenience which amazed us. Cap, Owen and Stetson followed the west bank for fifteen minutes to scare up a bag. Meg and I with Number One boy and a small *umphan*, a sort of general aide, followed downstream in the launch with the cameras set for action. We drifted, motor silent, the *umphan* watching for M'Moti and the two *bwanas* (white men). There was not a sound of bird or insect; then the *umphan* at the prow signaled M'Moti's position.

Coming up toward the east bank we saw a family of crocs lying on the beach with their jaws open. There was no movement from them, and they might have been tree logs, yet they are among the swiftest moving beasts on land or in water. I commented on their lack of resemblance to the alligator. Now I pressed the automatic switch of the camera, and as it whirred those open jaws snapped shut, the brutes whirled, each in its own length, and made for the water. Anyone within reach of those slashing tails would have been cut in two. Two shots rang out. Stetson and Owen stood on the beach, their rifles hot, and both reptiles were dead. It was an exciting moment; one I shall never forget.

We could hunt no longer then, for Stetson had duties. A consignment of raw natives had arrived from P.E.A. to be sent on to the Johannesburg mines. Their wives were with them and were being presented with gifts of necklaces, beads and pieces of bright calico print as compensation for the temporary loss of their husbands. Each man received a strip of calico also, and a bath rich with disinfectant. Twenty of them went off on foot to Louis Trechard. There, their first terrifying experience of white man's mechanical power would be the Kaffir Mail Express, to carry them to the pits of the Rand. Each had a six months' contract tied in his calico, and at the end of the time he would be free to return to his kraal, laden with trunks of calicos and tin billies gay with pictures of the royal family. These natives are conquering heroes on their return to the home village, but some succumb to the lure of Cape brandy spiked with carbibe and remain in the mines on renewed contracts, but five years is nearly always the limit for breathing gold dust. Phthisis and death seem the inevitable end if they stay too long. Cash money means nothing to the natives in the hinterland. We carried two pounds' weight of small coins, and later in one village I tried to buy some nuts, offering these tikis. The value of them is about threepence each. The whole village came to look at the tikis, but they were worth neither nuts nor mealies. It was Owen who thought up the jewelry idea. He drilled holes in the tikis, and then the women made trade faster than a white man will trade for gold nuggets. But I frequently used safety pins as a trade medium. We met village belles with thee or four of these most useful articles pushed through the lobes of the ear with quaint decorative effect, and apparently no bad results.

Smith gave us a fright as we stood on the edge of the cliff that led down from our host's *kopje*. We were saying adieu, and suddenly Cap's car, with Smith at the wheel, began to coast, gathering speed as it raced down the bluff. Like a projectile it reached the turn and swished out of sight; we could not tell whether he had gone over or round.

"Gone nuts," muttered Cap tersely, but when I drove my car very carefully down the slope, we saw Smith coming back on foot to warn and reassure us.

"Were you trying to demolish our precious car?" Cap demanded.

"I myself personally," commenced the absurd Cockney, "got my greatest thrill — that damned gear locked in neutral and I couldn't get it out." We thanked our lucky stars he had been able to keep the car, and himself, right side up.

We navigated the bed of the Limpopo, traveling through a sea of razor-edged grasses. Stetson's span of oxen awaited us and I watched the head car slowly submerge after those deliberate beasts. They came back for my machine. We forded on foot, and were lost in the forest of giant grass which reached far out on either bank. From then on, four of us by turn traveled on foot, for both cars were weighted to capacity with fuel, food and water, and they stuck constantly.

There were five ravines, old channels of the river, and the present course of the broad stream to be crossed by the aid of oxen. On the last bank, the black boys unhitched, turned and, before we could utter farewell or thanks, they were up to their waists in the river again. I'm sure they regarded us as mad people, and they were getting away from us.

Now we had to search for the opening of a trail, knowing that somewhere to the northeast of where we stood lay Chi Cuala-Cuala. At last, walking in single file with Cap and Meg leading, Smith steering one car and I the other, with Van and Owen sometimes ahead of everyone and sometimes behind, we crashed over strewn debris on the Limpopo bank, then began to make our way through dense jungle. We lost sight of the river beyond a heavy wall of immense trees, impenetrable even to the sun with their tangle of vines. Constantly we stopped to chop tangled growth that wound round the axles. Then suddenly we were in the clear, and bowled along over dry flats spotted with feathery-topped wattle trees and great bare boulders. We found we had traveled a mile and a half since leaving the river!

Toward sunset we struck a game trail intersecting our path at right angles. That brought us down to the river for our night's encampment, which Stetson had been recommending us to do when possible. The trail was well beaten and broad enough for the cars to travel with comparative ease. It was marked by the dried spoor of many animals. We parked the cars ten feet apart using the trunk of a huge tree as a wall between the radiators, and the branches gave a fine shelter. To complete the encircling wall, we piled the cases of fuel and on top placed provisions and chop boxes. A myriad of creeping things were upon the ground and one could not step without killing something.

Over all this we stretched a fifteen-by-twenty-foot tarpaulin, lashed it down and left the fourth wall up for the watch fire space, on the side farthest from the cans of gasoline. Meg put the Kaffir pot astride the flame to boil the peas; three hours later they sounded like lead pellets as they were poured into our enamel eating basins. We decided upon taking cooking lessons from some Kaffir matron when next we hit a kraal. That night each of us assumed a definite duty which we held to, more or less, for the early part of the drive. Owen and Smith undertook to repair tires; Cap had the care of the cameras, I crawled into my car and pulled down the special sleeping seats and chinked crevasses with our trench coats to insure comfort for Meg and myself. I fixed the other car also, and the men tossed for its sleeping use; the others dug hip holes in the gravel and slept beside the fire. We all rolled into our blankets, but nobody slept.

"Lions," whispered Meg as a thunderous, paralyzing roar seemed to vibrate the very structure of the car beneath us, and we clutched each other in our arms.

"Worst lion country in Africa," Stetson had warned us. One had jumped the eight-foot stockade around the cattle corral at his boma and jumped back with a donkey in its jaws. Even natives disappeared once in a while.

Shivers ran up and down our spines and I heard the men talking together. Sinister shadows now burdened the darkness, the shadows took form, and we saw a pair of eyes glaring from one side of the camp to the other. The fire had its effect as Van threw on more thornbush, and the eyes disappeared; then a jackal barked spasmodically.

"The distance makes it musical," I said to Meg, and my sister snorted disdainfully at me.

What a night! At last dawn came, trees became trees once more, the country took on a queer allure as that magic dawn wind filtered across the rippling water. Meg and I found a silver sandbar and washed away sleep and fatigue.

At six we were on the trail again for Chi Cuala-Cuala, and two hours after noon siesta we found ourselves on a hard beaten road fully two hundred feet wide. The brown bush was held back on either side by wide ditches, and as far as we could see ahead this surprising highway stretched unbroken. The smooth breast of a *kopje* rose shimmering in the torrid sun. Perhaps this road led to Mongoni's and then to Sabi. This surely was the two-hundred-mile road we had gleefully pointed out to Stetson as marked on an oil company's map of Mozambique. Stetson had scoffed but we had hoped, and apparently not in vain. The road lasted for a grand two miles.

That afternoon saw our approach to a native village. There was drought in Mozambique, and we could sense it as we struggled along, for we had already passed two kraals deserted by humans and animals alike before we came on a high thornbush stockage and found behind it about twenty terrified black folk. Twenty is the average population of a kraal. They wanted to run from the cars, but Smith managed the dialect and they became bold enough to remain, and bolder yet as the car engines went silent and stayed where we had stopped them.

A very brave young man approached, laid his hand on the hot radiator and fled screaming like a hyena, sucking at a burned hand. The entire population deserted after him, but all returned later and in single file they approached the cars until each had laid a finger on the car hood, which by now was quite cold. They smiled, delighted to have tamed *lo stutu*. Now was the moment for diplomatic rapprochement in the matter of food. But some woman among them found our rear vision mirror, and our dinner had to wait until this individual had made face contortions into the glass. Then more came up behind her to have a look, and they started a "touch the mirror" game to see whether there might be someone in it making faces.

It was Owen who provided a new interest. He got himself struck with the worst of the inevitable thornbush thorns. This is the "wait a minute," so named by the Boers. It is like a fish hook, and needs a special "wait a minute" method to free the catchee.

The next bit of excitement came from Smith and caused another exodus of natives, but not for so long. Smith was working at one of the cars, testing the engine. He let a native touch a sparkplug, the man received a shock which more than electrified him; he also ran howling, and the others after him. Later, when all was quiet and we had had our meal, this man begged a plug from Smith, which was readily given. Undoubtedly he is still trying to give his neighbors a shock from that inert piece of metal.

We made camp on the west side of the village, the cars now parked under the shade of a spreading boab tree, the squat trunk with its whitish-gray bark fully ten feet in diameter at the base. We had determined on resting here a few days, so we came to know these natives as both friendly and genial. We watched the arrival, too, of two natives traveling from another district. These men built a small watch fire on the further edge of the same kraal, outside the stockade. Unlike the cold nights to which we were becoming inured, this one was stifling; a scorching wind moaned in the branches over the car in which Meg and I lay. There was no sleep to be had.

Now, our French schooling had left a permanent influence on us as girls: Both of us went to Africa, and I through the other continents, breeched and booted, and frequently slept in those outfits, but we also carried each a lace-trimmed nightgown as a votive offering to our particular feminine Moloch. We wore the gowns that night. It must have been two in the morning when Meg decided on taking a stroll; booted but still in her chiffon and lace, she slipped out. There was not a sound in the kraal, and I smiled a bit as I watched her incongruously clad figure disappear behind a savage hut. I was not uneasy and I fell asleep. It cannot have been for long, although Meg was back beside me when we heard the cry: "Shimba! Shimba!"

That call that means "Lion!" roused our camp like a dousing of ice-cold water. I fell into my clothes and reached the group gathered round the chief, who pointed to Meg's small footprints circling the camp in the fine sand and not ten feet further out, but in a widening ring, was the deep spoor of a huge lioness. It had followed Meg round and back to the car. At our rear wheels there was a scuffed outline where the beast had lain down to sleep. Meg sobbed a bit with the shock of escape, although she had known nothing about her danger.

With rifles ready, we crossed the village to where the stranger natives' camp had been. The fire was out. The sand around told the tale; there was blood and the smooth lane made by a dragged body. It led north to a spot not two hundred yards from the village thorn barricade. A few scraps of a man's body remained. The second native must have fled, or maybe the scraps were of two people; or one might have been carried further away. The old lioness (the natives insisted it must be a female) had attacked and feasted, and then wandered over to our camp and followed Meg on her midnight stroll. But sated with the gruesome meal, the beast had lain down, then at dawn had gone to the mile-distant river for drink, for the spoor led us no further than the water's edge.

That day we hastily struck camp, left largesse of beads, safety pins and empty gasoline cans, and continued traveling, guiding ourselves by compass toward the boma of Mongoni, he who cheats the natives. He was Portuguese and spoke a broken English, and he needs a chapter to himself.

India, 1936

Egypt, 1936

1936

Java, 1936

ALOHA BAKER

Author of "CALL TO ADVENTURE"

PRESENTS

An Adventure Motion Picture Lecture

SPECTACULAR PICTURES
OF PEOPLE AND ANIMALS

ALOHA BAKER has taken her place in the front rank of the limited company of women explorers. "The World's Most Traveled Woman," a title frequently given to Aloha Baker, tells but half the story. Her expeditions have taken her over byways seldom covered by even the most intrepid male rovers.

This daring young woman has already covered Europe, Asia, Africa, North and South America. She has crammed enough adventure into her life to furnish several sensational novels, she has talked with Princes and untouchables, has been imprisoned by Chinese, created an honorary Colonel in the Red Army of Siberia and has seen Mussolini smile. It is a fact that she is as much at home among Luzon head-hunters, Javanese temple dancers, or Australian aborigines, as she is before a lecture audience.

Aloha Baker will tell you a story that will stir your imagination, a tale of daring and intrepidity that might challenge all the resources and courage of the most adventurous explorer.

Feeling "To Home" in the Bush

THERE was an official rondavel at the Mongoni boma. To reach the sacrosanct center where Meg and I could have a bath—the biggest treat of the stop-over—we passed through a kitchen kia. Mongoni, very polite, bowed me forward first. I topped him head and shoulders in the matter of height, but I pulled up sharp at a horrifying object hanging from under the kia eaves which a small person might not have seen. There dangled the raw, bloody fingers of a hand.

"Only monkey," murmured our too solicitous host; "very delicious meat."

At last he left us. The rondavel apartment was circled with shelves on which rested jars of specimens. We saw reptiles and peculiar bugs floating in yellow liquid contained in glass jars. We found ourselves no longer squeamish, so turned to the tub of hot water and shared its warmth, soap and a towel in perfect contentment, and forgot the creatures in the jars. We were interrupted by Smith's shout:

"Tea!"

Mongoni welcomed us on the verandah, surrounded by prize trophies of buffalo horns, rugs of lion skin and cheetah, and amid all this the host made an absurd figure in a pith helmet that rested on his fanlike ears. He really resembled an animated mummy, with shriveled skin and bones held together in a white cotton suit. But he was kindly, and his sharp little eyes glinted as he asked questions of our plans and adventures. He thought we were lunatics for undertaking such a thing, and perhaps we were.

We could see the whole boma from where we sat in rattan chairs and sipped delicious tea. I wished my Spanish had been Portuguese, for our host's English was a kindergarten variety, yet we managed a conversation. Round us were a cluster of low buildings of sun-baked mud, each having a verandah enclosed by bamboo screens. There was a strange leafless shrub bordering the paths; it had silver stems and branches bearing vividly pink wax-like blossoms. I could not understand the name Mongoni gave it, and we compromised on "pretty."

"Three years drought in Mozambique," explained our host, "only big game remains; the herds of gazelle and small animals have migrated to Rhodesia. It is a dangerous country now."

Seeing our genuine interest in his trophies, Mongoni pressed gifts on us until we were embarrassed, but Meg chose a beautiful cheetah skin, while I took a gorgeous gold and brown leopard skin.

"I myself personally shall have a lion," said Smith, who promptly used the huge bulk of it as a terrifying overcoat. Smith being the typical Cockney, with muscles like flexible steel wire, and with comical features entirely out of line, and with a doormat moustache, we had a hearty laugh at his antics. We had to be carefree at times or our experiences would have got us down.

Returning to the cars after tea for a siesta that was to last until dinnertime at the boma, Meg and I turned at the shrill laughter of children. I thought I saw a dozen small ivory-colored faces grinning behind us, and then amid a chatter of women's voices, they disappeared from sight. I determined to solve this household mystery when three or four other children peeked round the swinging service door into the large dining hall where the meal was served later. Stetson had given Cap a warning that conditions at Mongoni's were not those which we obtained at Pafuri. It seemed that Mongoni maintained five native wives, and I never succeeded in counting correctly the café au lait children. They looked all of an age and alike, and as we counted, Meg and I gave up in desperation at thirty-four. We think perhaps we numbered the same babies several times over, and that accounted for the monstrous figure.

The dining room was really a modish parlor, with furnishings that could be dated slightly prewar. There was an upright piano, its green velvet runner weighted by green pompoms; there were red plush picture frames from which ladies with hobble skirts looked down, and macramé-work tidies on the high-backed chairs set around a long table now spread with a white cloth and silver cutlery. There were assorted wines, and I tried not to think of what I might be eating. The meat was delicious and perfectly roasted. Natives, quite well trained, served an eight-course dinner.

It was astonishing, and Mongoni seemed pathetic as he begged again for news of the outside world. He told us he had come to Africa in 1914, foreswore his first leave after three years and thereafter, like many another European, the life of the outpost got him. He was resigned now to be king of all he surveyed.

In the evening we played ancient gramophone records on his rickety machine. Meg played what she could remember of pieces on the piano, which had many dumb keys.

In the days that followed we reciprocated the hospitality by having a picnic meal at our camp and showing Mongoni the still photographs of our travels. He looked at them over and over again. Cap and the men were stocking our cars with fresh supplies from the trading post, and Smith with Owen gave the engines a tremendous overhaul.

Mongoni expected a runner in from Sabi river who could be depended upon for news of the road. We secured the names of nine principal kraals which we should pass, and the approximate distances between them. The entire mileage from where we stood to the Massengena boma on the Sabi seemed to total up to one hundred and sixty miles. This we computed by guessing how far the runner could travel in one day, and calculating from the number of times the black boy swung his arm in the arc of the sun from horizon to horizon. It was complicated but amazingly accurate.

We would have to be careful; all streams between Mongoni's and the Sabi were reported dry, water could be obtained only at the kraal water holes, and we might come on a hostile tribe. But the runner was encouraging, for he thought it possible to take *lo stutu* through the bush as long as we equipped ourselves with a good saw and an axe with which Mongoni's trade supplied us. We paid in sterling.

Mongoni's parting gifts were a tin of coffee, cigarettes for Owen and Smith, the only two of the party who smoked, some tea, four gallon cans of elephant fat for Meg's kitchen equipment, and two quarters of olive oil. His Number One boy brought up a long and heavy cross-cut saw; also one large and several smaller axes, the last so Meg and I could handle them. The sight of these things started Smith into a recital which began:

"I myself personally think it mad," and with each spaced word he wrapped some article of his own in his lion skin.

"What's that?" said Cap. "We are going through and you are going with us, if we saw out every step of the trail."

Cap consulted Mongoni's sundial, the runner raised his gleaming black arm in the direction of the Sabi, and Cap checked the bearings on his compass, marking the course on its face. That was the last of the preparations for the second lap of the journey.

The fly-sand bed of the Tokuai river rose up as our first major obstacle after some days of travel which we had considered hard enough. This made agonies of labor. We were forced to portage the cases of gasoline, and all provisions and equipment across the three-quarter-mile expanse. The sun blazed as we put our shoulders to the cars and pushed and hauled them over one at a time. On the far bank we used our spades to shovel out a trail so the cars could be pushed up the steep incline. That crossing took us seven hours.

The engines were roaring as we plowed a single path through bush to the first kraal, Masekele. There was not a native in sight; eight or ten round thatched huts circled a baked mud clearing. Empty calabashes lay around, and a Kaffir pot simmered with food in it, over smoldering ashes. The automobiles had terrified everyone. Being a woman, considered less likely to be thought harmful than a man, despite Kipling, I advanced cautiously to the nearest *mooti* (hut). I called softly, using words Smith and Van had taught me, and displayed a length of biltong.

I could hear commotion inside the huts, and at last a tall and quite aged man, naked but for his skimpy buckskin apron and an ebony circlet on his head, advanced slowly. I smiled. That finished him. He turned and fled back to the huts, but shrill laughter greeted him and the decision seemed to whet his courage. He appeared again and offered a calabash in which I should place the meat. After some gesticulating I got over the idea that we wanted the food and water and were not giving some away. The Chief bellowed to his people and the women rushed out, stared at me and then resumed their corn stamping and the tending of fires. Presently Owen herded six huge women with large calabashes on their heads of closely curled hair, and shouting "lo mansi, lo mansi" (water), he started them in procession making a rhythmical parade to the water hole. Van brought up the rear with his hunting knife in one hand and his rifle in the other. On later trips he substituted his rawhide *sjambok* for the knife.

The Chief now offered us both hands in a gesture of welcome as is their custom of friendship, and within an hour we had camp set right in the middle of the *shamba*, appropriating the shade of the only tree within the five-foot lion stockade of thornbush. We found that the height of stockade varied in every kraal. Smith got together some useful-looking natives to gather us wood, spread tarpaulins, pump tires, which hey thought fun, and to lift the cases. They seemed to work from curiosity, for they examined minutely each thing they touched. In payment each received a pinch or two of salt. We turned on the car headlights as a display which thrilled and terrified at the same time, and Meg and I saw our one precious lipstick, saved against return to civilization, pass from mouth to mouth and disappear on the acreage of women's mouths which it had to cover. We only needed to show those women once what it was for.

At this kraal we inveigled a black boy to act as guide for us to the next kraal, which was Matsumbi, promising him rich reward of varied kinds. He was worth it.

There were ranging hills and high plateaus, and the cars were pulled by our power much more often than we used the motors. We dared not expend too much gasoline on inclines we knew could not be conquered even by these engines which were proving extraordinary. We had the feeling that we were climbing constantly to a mesa of great extent. For several miles the path was strewn by fallen trees, felled, as the guide explained, not by tornado but by a passing herd of elephants. We hacked and sawed a way through them for the cars, while the guide was terribly nervous. Elephants maddened with thirst in drought-ridden country are a very real danger. I had visions of finding the mysterious valleys of elephant tusks and bones where elephants go to die, according to legend. I never did. My theory is that dying elephants trek off into the impenetrable privacy of the jungle where their bones lie undisturbed and finally decay back into the dankness of Mother Earth.

More and more we became certain that we were in the path of elephants. We came to a deserted kraal which the guide did not seem to recognize. We did not stop in the *shamba*, but camped near the dry bed of a creek. We knew by the blow holes fifteen to twenty feet deep in the sand that elephants had passed that way, for the elephants blow these pits in seeking water. The guide persuaded us to break camp and move back within the deserted *shamba*, and we build up roughly the broken stockade. We used the water we carried, for we could find no water hole with a mile radius of the kraal.

We slept, and were awakened by the trumpeting thunder of an elephant herd. The guide was in near panic and urged us to set fire to the rotting thatch of the huts to scare the herd away. We had fired three huts, those well away from the cars and the extra fuel, and then realized that when inhabited by natives the smoke of native fires keeps snakes away, but now the ground near the flaming *mootis* was literally carpeted with snakes. Our fires were driving them from the thatch. We made for the cars. Next morning we saw a swathe fifteen feet wide torn through the jungle where the elephants had detoured. Our fires cannot have burned up much too soon.

At Matsumbi we began to feel badly the effects of the drought. The natives were reluctant to barter for food or water, and the water hole was three hours' travel from the kraal. Again we did with the water we carried, while Van took a few native women as carriers, and made for the water supply. Cap and Owen took rifles and cartridges and Owen shot a buck, which was unexpected. When the two men appeared with the game the natives screamed with excitement, and the uproar grew as the men stood by with sharpened knives to skin the animal. It was here we learned how to cut the meat into the long narrow strips, to be hung from the branches of trees in the sun, there to dry into biltong.

At Matsumbi we discovered that one of our big assets was Meg, who had long hair, dark as mine was fair. To the natives who rarely had seen a white person, Meg stood out amongst us who were predominately blond. She found she was allowed to fondle babies, some of whom were really adorable; she could discuss culinary topics by signs, grunting and laughter. This gift of Meg's brought to us considerable native assistance which we could hardly have achieved otherwise.

Three weeks' travel from Matsumbi we reached the third kraal of which we had the name; this was Chikueza. The edge of the bush here showed scars for a fresh clearing, and we waited, for the soil of the compound was newly turned, and there were only three *mootis*, with no one about. Our guide left us here with the peculiar abruptness of being here now and gone in the next second. Then we watched the Chief of Chikueza approach along the trail, three wives in his wake, each bearing on her head cone-shaped baskets of mealies. They were evidently moving in from an old *shamba*.

These people proved to be very friendly right from the start since the roar of the cars had not alarmed them. We made camp, and it was while here that I repaired some torn shorts with one of the three needles left in a limited sewing kit. The native women gathered round, intrigued by the steel needle. One, bolder than the others, begged with expressive gestures for this precious implement of civilization. I shooed her away. But in twenty minutes she had come back to show me a large triangular tear in her wrap-around buckskin skirt. Her ingenuity won her the needle.

Chief Chikueza was able to keep up a fairly coherent conversation with Van, and the result was an offer to take us on a buffalo hunt. The Chief had evidently never had a female on a hunt before; he ignored me so utterly that I felt like a disembodied spirit when his glance fell on me for he certainly assumed that I was not to be seen. He christened Owen "Big Noise," and became his bosom friend; and Van, through whose good offices the whole thing had been planned, just tagged along so far as the Chief was concerned. But we got our buffalo.

Throbbing Tom Toms

CHIEF CHIKUEZA proved to be a remarkable tracker and hunter. By the hoof impressions on the trail of a buffalo he was able to tell whether the animal was a bull, how large it was, how swift, about what age, and how many hours or days since the beast had passed that way. When another path intercepted ours and the spoor direction was not entirely clear, Chikueza took from a fur pouch at his waist a handful of carved bones and talked to them until I felt myself back in Oxford, Mississippi, on a Saturday night; then he scattered the bones across the last clear impress of spoor. The position of the bones indicated the direction the animal had followed — due east. We turned east. At the next halt, Chikueza pulled a hair from the magic pouch and held it out in the breeze. Again the direction was east. Two more hours of hard walking brought us to the edge of the grassy pan of a dried-up lake bed, but there was the dampness of recent water in the middle of it. Far across an expanse of tall waving grass we saw a black buffalo grazing. We waited until the beast lay down, and through the sedges we could only see the hump of his great shoulders. Chikueza checked wind direction, this time by kicking up sand, for we had to keep the wind in our faces if we were to stalk our prey within shooting distance.

Owen, who is an excellent shot, fired when the Chief told him. The buffalo reared up; I raised my .303, aimed, pulled the trigger. The animal leaped, then landed stiff-legged on all fours, stood still and glared. We were close enough to hear his snorting breath. Owen fired again and got the beast square between the eyes. Our first—and last— buffalo sank among the reeds.

On the list of kraals was Tekuai, but somehow we missed it altogether. We struck another village, secured water, and by compass we reached Mazatuani after five days of heavy travel. This place was deserted. We shouted out the Shangaan words of good will, but there was only a ghastly silence. We could hear the dry rattle of reeds as a black mamba reared a hissing head and slithered over the thatches. Before the *mootis* lay pestle and mortars, much as are used for pounding mealies. Small logs were neatly arranged for fire, but the gray ashes were cold when we felt them. The silent kraal gave us a vague fear, for without native assistance there was little change of our finding a water hole. These holes are always some distance from a village as a measure of protection, since lions like to share the use of such primitive wells.

"Probably no death is more horrible than that by thirst," said Meg. I knew she was quoting from an old lesson book we both had studied but—

"Shut up," said Cap.

I stooped where I saw a piece of metal; it was part of a rusted old slave chain which had been filed through. We wondered if some Arab trader had passed this way, or if there had been a plague; but there were no skeletons or human bones.

As we had to camp and rest, we made a fire, and heard again the trumpeting of elephants. We built several more fires and larger ones. We examined our supply of gasoline and oil, and nobody spoke when the meager amount had been totted up.

Not far from this camp our way went through a grove of slender saplings. We started to cut them, but found that they lay down of themselves in our passage across, and sprang up again after the cars had gone by, so we used the cars again, but we crashed against hidden boulders and got into fly sand over and over again. Then we spent one whole day portaging our stuff across five hundred feet of sand and almost literally carried the car. The heat was intolerable.

Meg and I were fined down as the men, our muscles taut as drawn steel, and it seemed our endurance was unending, but that night when standing on the radiator of my car to reach an end of stretching tarpaulin, I fell to the ground and could not rise. I was just too tired. Our outfit was strictly teetotal on the trail, but we carried one treasured flask of wine given us by M'Noti Stetson. The others thought I had fainted, and maybe I had for a moment or two, but I was aware enough to hear one of the boys say:

"Hell, there goes our bottle of wine!" Meg held a small tin with some of the port to my lips. I swallowed and felt better.

In the next days we came to a broad belt of heavy green forest which confronted us across the *veldt*; it was too wide to detour around, so we chopped a pathway with only inches left to spare in getting the cars through. The land of Mozambique is one of distinct belts, the vegetation changing in a matter of miles. For instance, one day we crashed through a phantom forest where there were fire-blackened tree trunks and soot-covered sand. The cars, under their own power, plunged and pitched into many holes. Again we came on a forest where shells of trees stood with the core eaten out by white ants, and these fell and crumbled at a touch of the hand before our astonished eyes. We passed through a mahogany forest where the enormous branches had been snapped off by elephants. We had to saw and hack a way through brush, while in the further distance we could see gray backs of elephants going at an easy pace. That heartened us, for our water was getting very low, and since the elephants appeared to be content, it showed there must be water somewhere within reach.

We found the water hole and replenished our supply but we were really only advancing by inches. We gave up all thought of Sabi, Cairo, civilization and the future, and bent our energies to the immediate goal set for the day. We tried to make the going as regular as possible, with two stops a day for food, but there would be twenty stops in twelve hours to patch tires and tubes ripped by wigs of mahogany and thorns. I filtered water through a bag of sand, which left the liquid a milky shade but freed of particles, and, we hoped, of live things. Mealtimes became a weary monotony of boiled peas and more muddy water. It was an unappetizing diet, yet kept us going. None of us became actively ill.

There was now a distinct definiteness about the trail. We felt we must be nearing Matz'Ketze if we were still on the right track. Along this path we saw the unique traps we had been told the Shangaan set for small animals. We were careful not to disturb these.

A circle of smooth twigs is sunk in the ground, a springy branch is pulled down by a string tied to it, usually a length of tough vine. The other end of this is a loop. The noose is placed over the circle of twigs and a loose end is baited with a piece of biltong The animal steps into the circle to eat the bait, disturbs the loop, which is jerked into the air by the springy bough, and the little beast is hanged.

There came now a patch of cultivated ground with dried mealie stalks showing, so we began our advance, using a method we had proved got superior service in the kraals where the natives had been growing more suspicious of us as we penetrated further into the bush. We knew our advance to the lion stockade was being watched from all angles, so we put on speed and rushed that compound, throttles open, motors roaring, and the sirens screaming. Women shrieked, snatched up their children and fled before this strange menace. With the engines switched off, and our camp already being set up, the inhabitants began to come back.

Matz'Ketze was a prosperous village. There were flocks of skinny chickens, and we saw several herd of cattle and a corral of goats. At least twenty women, each with a baby on her back, were stamping mealies in huge mortars carved from tree trunks. A group of quite young girls were cracking nuts which were new to me. They seemed to be a cross between a Brazil nut and a miniature coconut. The meat was succulent and pleasant in flavor, but I could not make barter for a long time, not until Owen had time to drill holes in more tikis.

Our supply of oil was running very low and my car was in bad shape. A hole had been rammed in the crankcase which we had closed with a plug of the mahogany wood. The hole continued to leak, oozing out a precious drop at a time.

The runner from Chi Cuala-Cuala passed through this village while we rested. We clipped a note to Mongoni in the split fork of the runner's staff, and in this asked the Commandant to send us back some oil. We waited ten days at Matz'Ketze and got no reply and no oil, and no runner came. Then, taking a chance on the oil and stocking up with kerosene from the Matz'Ketze homesteaders, which they seemed to have in quantity for burning in trade lamps, we pushed on to Shogmani, carrying also as much food as they would trade us. We feared it was not nearly enough for our need but we could get no more.

Smith walked ahead to the next kraal, hoping to make preparations for our coming. "There is not a man in sight about the place," he reported; "must all be off at the mines, but there's something funny about the whole place—the girls would not talk." Smith knew this lingo.

We camped, and the women gathered round, but when we attempted to bargain for food and water we came up against an iron wall of refusal. We offered valuable empty gasoline cans, magnificent gilt and silver safety pins in assorted sizes, also some dulled and discarded razor blades which we had saved. Nothing moved these women to friendship.

Young Van became enraged. Being a Boer youth, he knew how to deal with native stubbornness, so we let him take the lead. He lifted his *sjambok*, which he had carried around since he joined us, snapped it savagely, then barked out orders for food in his kitchen Kaffir. When none of the women moved, he wheeled round and shoved a girl into the cattle corral.

"Milk!" Van commanded. The girl obeyed, and we drank the liquid thirstily, then ate plentifully. Those women went on tiptoe as they came near Van, and even to me the lad seemed to have grown a foot taller.

That evening, round a huge camp fire, we took out our guitars and the uke for the first time in weeks. The black women listened without emotion to our American jazz airs, the Owen took the instrument and played some Cuban folk music, the cadence of which is definitely African. As they heard "Chaparita," those natives rose from squatting, and commenced to dance. This was Shobmani, the village of women who never before had seen a white woman, and whose men folk were all away at the mines.

It was extraordinary to watch them; they swayed forward, the retreated with teeth gleaming against the firelight, their bronze bare faces and torsos glinting, their nostrils dilating and the leather wraps that clothed their hips swinging with the movement. Behind them was blackest night; the flames roared higher and I looked at the faces of our party near me.

There was Meg, her eyes wide with wonder and her lips parted as she hummed a little accompaniment to the melody; Cap had a smile that showed his artistic appreciation of this whole weird setting. Owen's grin was cynical as he beat out the melody over and over again, and the angular young Dutch face of Van was hard to read. Smith sat looking superior and austere, fingering the straggly hair on his upper lip, which had once been a dapper mustache. I was electrified when I saw him dash in amongst the women and drag Cap with him. Those two men capered and danced like savages; every now and then, Smith, the Cockney, would yell out, "Hoot, mon!"

It was ridiculous, but these writhing black figures touched a dormant wildness in each of us. I heard stolid Van begin to beat time on empty gasoline can, then the dancers caught the melody and shrilled out verses of their own composing. In the strange dance movements the women slapped their toes on the ground, then brought their heels down with a flat tonal thud. I found myself plucking the strings of my guitar, swaying and singing in the same vibrant strain.

Weariness of body sent us to our camp, and by dawn I heard Van snapping his *sjambok* lash and rounding up those women, with gas cans and calabashes balanced on their head rings of coiled grass. The water hole was no more than a round trip of seven miles.

The day passed and Van with his herd of water carriers had not returned. At intervals we blew the siren of Cap's car; then I took to firing two precious shots at three-minute intervals. At last we heard a police whistle; each of us carried one strung round our necks throughout the whole adventure. I fired again and the whistle blew again, but it was quite a full hour before Van struggled into camp trailed by the water women. He was stammering with rage and faint with fatigue.

"Those verdompt women lost the trail on the way back. Instead of seven miles I've been seventeen, and I bet they did it on purpose!"

Fed, and left to sleep, Van was his own masterful self in other day. And then our journey commenced again. We left loaded up with the precious equipment of water.

A path beaten by native feet led at variance with the compass direction indicated, and we hoped this path was right; but the trail suddenly ended where dried mud of a pan's surface looked like a battlefield pitted with shell holes. Again elephants frantic for water, had expended lung power in search of something to drink. About ten different trails led from a second dry pan—evidently not so long dry, for the abutting forest had not yet turned a drab brown. Meg sought the shade of a mahogany tree and seated herself where an ant hill reached as high as the lower branches.

"Run, Meg!" the alert-eyed Van screamed. He was just in time, for as Meg ran the vile head of a snake reared from the ant hill, then the vivid green coils of a huge mamba detached itself from a branch and lasted itself out of sight in the undergrowth.

The trail became fainter. We cut down on our water rations; there was no more laughter and little talk. For the first time we had become really apprehensive of thirst. The trail bore west and, most certainly, we should have been steering north. We saw no sign of the padding footsteps of an inter-kraal runner, and only one thing was cheering: There was a slight descent in the irregularity of the terrain, and the vegetation was increasingly jungle-like once more. Lion and leopard spoor became thick. That surely meant water.

Cap and Van went ahead to trace the path. We waited in the open with our lips now parched and cracking. We chewed dry corn to help in keeping our mouths a little moist.

"In the ravine only a sand drift," reported the two men on their return. It seemed that somewhere we had taken the wrong trail.

I felt I must think this out alone, so I took my rifle and whistle and went to the empty gulch to settle myself on a boulder. The cool evening breeze would blow up presently and help. In the silence around me I became aware of eyes beyond another boulder. I jerked to life and fired, then blew my whistle. The noises startled the giant cat which lurked there; I heard a snarl, then saw a tawny gold-and-black body leap back to the jungle growth.

Cap came running. I think he was glad my aim had been bad; he had never recovered from the death of that first springbok, but I regretted I had not had the camera, because the leopard was there long enough to get a shot.

I have never suffered before nor since as I did the next day. The sun scorched, and once I sat down feeling ready to give up; then Meg and Cap came pushing my car, with Smith steering it as he walked and pushed as well. I got up to give a hand. We reached an expanse of low palmettos, a circular clearing with ring marks on it, and in the middle there was water. We forgot caution and dropped to our knees and lapped the slimy, putridly saline liquid. It was vile, but it was water. We gathered wood for our watch fire and saw a flock of several hundred doves whir into the clearing to settle by what was left of the once large lake. A second drove of "Go-away birds" filled the air and took possession of the precious fluid. We had filled our containers. After moonrise there came a stealthy stirring all around us, and once there was a mighty roar. In the morning we counted spoor of bushbuck, waterbuck, cheetah, kudu, leopard, eland and hyena, and since there was the last, there must have been lion. The water was roiled and muddied, but I filtered it through the sand bag, and we were ready to start again.

The gas now was petering out, and I put the last drop or two of oil into the crankcase myself. According to calculations, the Sabi should only be twenty miles north from where we were. We held a conference, and Cap and Van proposed to strike ahead to get the Portuguese Commandant to send back supplies and a trek wagon.

"Don's try to ride in the cars," said Cap, as he went out of sight. But the trail opened onto a smooth stretch, almost as smooth as the wide road of two miles' length which we had hoped was going to be two hundred. The lagging cars began to move under their own power, and Meg and Smith could not resist temptation. They started to ride, the car lurched to the side and stopped dead; we watched the left rear wheel roll along a slight declivity before us, collapse pitifully with the hub rolling a few feet further.

Smith scouted ahead and found a water hole. He brought us this good news, and then volunteered to stay with the disabled car, in which we packed the cameras and valuable film, transferring what fuel there was and same equipment to the other car. We left Smith provisions, such as they were, together with a rifle, automatic, ammunition and all the cigarettes we could find among the things, and help him to rig up a shelter and collect wood for his fire. While we were still working a runner came from the north carrying two gallon kerosene cans slung over his shoulder; the white ends of a message fluttered from his staff. Cap wanted Meg and me to walk, with the runner to guide us, to Massengena. Cap wrote that he believed only one car could get through by driving a roundabout trail to the northeast, and he designated Owen as driver for that. He did not know about the wheel disaster.

Gomani, the last village before the Sabi, was reported to be only two hours ahead. We waved to Owen as he went off, then left Smith reluctantly and, with a small gourd of water and our automatics as our only baggage, Meg and I set off for Gomani, walking as smartly as we could, but we had to ask the runner guide to travel slowly.

White Men with Black Morals

GOMANI was squalid and poverty-stricken, and there were only three *mootis*, built with a tree as center. No cattle were in view, no children, and no moth eaten dogs, and we were apprehensive when we saw no women around, although we might have expected that where there was no cultivation, since the women are the farmers of the kraals. Eight men lolled listlessly about watching scraggly chickens scratch for grubs in the litter of the compound. Owen arrived and managed to trade a gasoline can for two roosters. We roasted them in another can, ate one, so tough we could hardly swallow it, and sent its mate back by runner to Smith.

Meg and I set out again, close on the heels of our Massengena guide, and Owen started the car for the more open but much longer trail. We could see river-bordered jungle ahead and our path descended rapidly for an hour, confirming our belief that we had been on a plateau since the ascent at Chi Cuala-Cuala.

It was perhaps three o'clock by the sun when our runner stopped and pointed across the stretch of land below us. On a distant *kopje* we could make our dots of thatch, and a piece of red, white and green bunting showed up clearly. That was the Portuguese flag at the Sabi post known as Massengena.

We had two hours more of continuous walking before we saw Cap running to meet us. Behind him came a corpulent little Senhor, Cammandant Jose Maria Fernandes de Silva de Souza, known with a rather terrifying familiarity to the natives as Wafa Wafa.

We sank gratefully into wicker chairs on his verandah as he ordered servants to bring us glasses of crystal clear water. The sun poised on the rim of the bush; the sky was molten, swirling gold; a flat-topped tree stood out like an etching. A tall negro stood as though carved in an ebony statue seen in silhouette, his raised arms and hands poised above a set of big tom-toms. Half the sun's disk was gone, the rest seemed to lose balance and topple off the world; then the staccato tattoo of drums vibrated, deepened, rumbled across the veldt and floated over the broad, silver expanse of the Sabi river. It was wonderful. We relaxed in peace, glad to emulate Wafa Wafa, whose native name means "the little fat man indisposed to exertion."

A runner was dispatched to Smith with coffee, tea and other provisions and a message that relief would come to him soon. We set ourselves to wait, first for Owen, and then for Van, who had volunteered on a courageous mission. Alone, but for one native, and with a rifle, a sack of mealie, some hardtack and a water calabash, Van had set out to walk one hundred and ten miles northwest to Umtali in Rhodesia, a white settlement. He was to return on the monthly trek wagon bringing spare parts and fuel.

On this trip Van went through Africa's greatest elephant country; he passed cow elephants and their young, and took his rest periods under mahogany trees, but he made the trip in record time.

Meanwhile, content that Smith was all right, and satisfied that Owen would get the car through, we gave ourselves up to the enjoyment of the moment.

Wafa Wafa told us his story; he kept the fantastic and unreal narrative in the third person until we found out the secret. A young Lisbon business man, he told us, accepted a post with the Mozambique Company as Commandant to the Sabi territory. With his quite young wife he set out on a great adventure to make their fortunes. There were three years of living in a mud-wattle dwelling, collecting hut taxes, punishing witch doctors, sending records by runner, fever-aid dispensing, repairing thatch, and looking for the monthly trek wagon. The little home-loving wife, broken in spirit and health, went back to her family. He went to Portugal for his six months' leave, but luring Africa had him by the throat. He left wife and home and came back.

Here Wafa Wafa strummed pudgy fingers idly against the strings of his native guitar and looked wistfully over the Sabi. He fooled neither Meg nor myself in his third-person camouflage, and as we discussed it later, neither of us thought he was interested in returning to wife and homeland. We found out why.

Leaving our sleeping rondavel in the morning, we surprised a domestic scene on the verandah corner. It was the essential bit Senhor the Commandant had left out of his story. He sat now, garbed in creased white shirt and duck trousers, overlapping the chair with his bulk, and at his feet on a length of golden matting squatted a beautiful young creature, African in every ebony curve, but with features so fine that but for her vitality, she might have been an exquisite carving. She spoke rapidly, and waved her hand at the semicircle of natives squatting on the ground before the pair.

Wafa Wafa saw us, gave a sharp Shangaan command and the circle of blacks vanished, but the ebony human doll remained. The Senhor was embarrassed, but Meg and I came forward and proffered a greeting.

She was Maringa, a true black beauty, her features not negroid in the slightest, but more Arabic. Her hips were tightly wrapped in a fine yellow silk *shimba*; on her close cropped-hair she wore a circle of fine white beads, the crown of an exalted Chief's wife. Wafa Wafa commanded Sabi and Massengena, but Maringa ruled Wafa Wafa. She adored him, but was very conscious of her power and position since she had stepped into the place of the white Bibi. Coy, sparkling with wit and possessing a sense of humor, and with beautiful changes of clothing fashioned by the Goanese storekeeper on his little American-made sewing machine, Maringa conducted herself as a most fascinating queen. Her wizened old mother informed me that Wafa Wafa had paid five pounds for her lovely daughter. The old hag was inordinately proud of the situation.

Maringa's great talent was dancing. Her music came from a Portuguese guitar played by a native who carried a melody on it, while another kept the tom-tom beat. This was L'kona as we had never seen it before. Maringa planted her feet firmly, kept shoulders and arms gracefully motionless, and made her vibrant torso twirl in a peculiarly rhythmic motion.

Meg and I found a pool of the Sabi in which we could enjoy a private bath. Maringa would not be outdone by white Bibis. She came with us, accompanied by umphans carrying a tin trunk. When these male serfs withdrew she produced squares of bright silks used for shimbas; then, exploring the trunk further, she found a huge cake of bright purple soap so violently scented that fish and crocodiles withdrew from the vicinity. Her ablutions over, the soap and shimba cloths were replaced in the trunk, the umphans reappeared, and the ritual of the morning was completed.

Each afternoon Meg and I spent a siesta hour on a high embankment by the river. We discovered five brilliantly colored fish holding themselves against the stream and studied them, plainly seen under the clear water, with interest. We proved that they listened to music. Always we had our guitars with us; when the music stopped the fish floated away, when we played again softly they swam back. The Senhor did not know the name of the species, but he came to watch when we brought Cap to see the curious performance.

Cap, Meg and I had two immediate anxieties. The two runners came in and reported locating a broken *lo stutu*, but no Smith; and Owen had not yet appeared.

One afternoon the light was waning when an uproar came from the native compound below the boma enclosure. The noise sent everyone rushing to the main verandah. The natives reported a roaring demon traveling without oxen, propelled by magi, and glimpses of a devil which made it go. They had fled before it.

Maringa, standing very erect by Wafa Wafa, was translating the Commandant's assurances that the people would not be harmed. This was the white man's *lo stutu* which had come from the end of the world on the southern horizon, Chi Cuala-Cuala.

A sputtering roar came nearer, the swarm of blacks fidgeted and chattered. A young hunter told how he had seen *lo stutu* in the forest path and had hidden himself. It was a huge bug; it droned with the noise of many elephants; it plunged and reared like a lion; it climbed over fallen trees, howling in a fearful range, it had one eye that glared. A bwana with bloodshot eyes and hair on his head and face like yellow metal clung tightly to a stick to keep from being thrown by the beast, which had a hollow back. All game fled before its advance.

Wafa Wafa laughed heartily at this, and Cap and I were relieved to recognize Owen in the description, for no one else had hair like molten metal.

Just at sundown, we sighted the metal bug with the fire spitting eye, coming more slowly than an umphan can walk, traveling on a wide trail between the forest edge and the kopje. Owen found the path, the engine coughed, sputtered and roared to the top of our knoll.

"I was determined to bring the verdompt thing in under its own power," said Owen, and stepped down.

He was a sight. Maringa, brave as she was, shrank behind Wafa Wafa's pot-bellied form. *Lo stutu* was ferocious-looking. A cloud of smoke rose from the hood; there came the nauseating odor of burned bananas, sizzling elephant fat and hot oil, and the stench of burned bearings. The final backfire had thrown off a cloud of blue smoke and white steam.

"I used crushed bananas in the differential," said Owen; "that's that smell. I had elephant oil and olive oil as lubricants, and they're not too good for any car, even an auto like this." Owen hustled off to bathe and shave, and Cap with him to give him a haircut.

Smith was now our continued worry, and he turned up hours later. The runners had missed him and he could give no coherent account of having got off the trail. He was staggering as he came and we ran to give him support. His shorts were thorn-torn, his flesh scarred, his face sun-blistered under days of whisker growth. That he had a touch of sun and bush-madness was very evident.

"No cigarettes left," he croaked; "My throat's raw with smoking dry leaves."

Smith was in a pitiful state, and the condition of his throat was serious. We had to wait for Van and the trek wagon, the spare parts and provision, for we were a drain on the Massengena supplies even now. We were terribly anxious about the films and equipment Smith had had to leave behind, but we just had to wait and put in time as best we could.

Elephant Hunt

I WENT hunting with Owen, and the Senhor delegated Bandi to accompany us. Bandi was a splendid specimen of the Shangaan. He looked as though built of polished ebony, with broad shoulders, lithe muscles that rippled as he moved and limbs built for speed. He had an alert eye and a quick brain, for his kind, and always was neat-looking in a brilliant limbo of peacock green, a flamboyant splash of color which could be distinguished from afar. Our hunting was in no way designed for a real safari, but we stalked big game and saw herds of gazelle, so we obtained some fresh meat.

The congregation of game here was quite out of the ordinary. The extensive territory overtaken by drought had been deserted for this fertile valley through which the Sabi flowed crystal clear and free. In other colonies the holocaust amongst the wild animals was going on; hundreds of safaris, with the hunters armed with high-powered rifles and new schemes for driving the poor brutes, made their hunting no better than a slaughter. It seemed that the big game would be exterminated if something drastic were not done by officials. Mozambique was closed to hunting except for the Commandants and natives. Three seasons of drought made the animal concentration great. The scent of water attracted the animals from rain-starved areas. Here they were safe from those hunters who turn their sport into wholesale killing for greed.

Bandi told us of hundreds of elephants browsing to the north; of eland and cheetah cat; of sable antelope, lion and droves of buffalo. We believed him. At the boma we lived almost exclusively on the fresh meat of kudu, known as Africa's royal game. We were very conscious, despite Wafa Wafa's unvarying, courteous hospitality, that we were five more mouths to feed.

We saw hundreds — I might better write thousands — of crocodiles polluting the streams and sunning themselves on narrow strips of beach. They made bathing exciting, and crossing the river by daylight thrilling and dangerous too; and at night the infested waters meant suicide for anyone who ventured in them. But despite this, we swam daily in the river.

We had been trying to persuade Wafa Wafa to detail natives to portage our equipment to the north bank, from where our new start must be made. His indolence and his association with Maringa had lost him his control over the blacks. The boys refused to wade stream, until one day when Smith, feeling well enough to join the swimming, yet fearful of losing his double set of false teeth, carefully placed the teeth on a safe rock overlooking the water. The natives, who invariably came to see the swimming, caught sight of them and were intrigued by them. Meg, who had been quick in mastering the dialect, was asked: "What magic has the bwana over the crocodiles?" Thinking of the portage for which we hoped, Meg explained:

"The magic teeth are a guard against the crocodiles. If a crocodile came near, the magic teeth would jump into the river, grow bigger and bigger and eat up all the crocs!"

"Hey!" shouted Smith as he came to reclaim his property, and he mumbled with sunken gums:

"Next thing you know they'll try to steal my teeth — what do you think I myself personally would do without them?" Meg had no reply, but natives volunteered there and then for the portage which, after all, we were not to need.

At the foot of the kopje cliff there was a "croc slip," a narrow line of breach where crocodiles basked in sunshine. Across the river was a lagoon and sand bar with dense vegetation, the bar bordered by a thick fringe of reeds. Here hippopotamuses rippled the water and poked up ugly snout from the undergrowth to stare at us with pig eyes. We were not to see rhinoceros until near Nairobi, and then, fortunately, not at close quarters.

In the third week at Massengena a safari of native boys forded the river coming south. They carried heavy burdens of elephant ivory. The signal tom-tom rolled, the two military boys of the post and the Commandant's personal attendants bustled around. In crumpled white linen, Wafa Wafa took his seat. Maringa crouched at his feet, the two uniformed black boys stood to attention and several scores of people from the kraal crowded up to the compound fence. This was the formal acknowledgment of custody of ivory. It precluded the arrival of Bwana Snyder, who, I found, was professional hunter for the Mozambique Company lessees of this Portuguese East African colony. Bwana Snyder was on his way to Massengena; he was now delayed stalking a bull tusker in the hills, but the Senhor Commandant would receive the ivory into safe keeping.

A few days later Wafa Wafa pointed to a trail clearing on the far side of the river:

"Snyder comes — listen!"

In the silence we strained our ears toward the direction in which he pointed; then, faint but clear, came the creak of wagon wheels, the crack of a whip and shouts of boys. The sounds seemed as though coming through a long tunnel.

"Let's sit down and wait for them," I suggested. "I'm anxious to meet Snyder."

Wafa Wafa laughed at me. "He will not be here for two days.

I was incredulous, but had to believe the marvel of bush *ondes* or sound waves which come over the ether, unaltered in tone though diminished in volume, by transmission over forty-eight hours of territory. The sounds are "small" but entirely distinct. I could imagine it possible to train the auditory nerves to tune in an actual series of speech tones if due direction were followed, and the parties knew the experiment was being tried.

Snyder arrived when Wafa Wafa had predicted, and encamped on the far side of the river. We plunged into the water waist deep and forded over to his camp. He was a lean, sinewy Boer, typical of his profession, with face and arms tanned a rich brown. He wore heavy twilled clothing, a battered slouch hat, his cartridge belt was full and his footgear was of stout hand-sewn *veldtschoen*. His partner was named Muller, a mild youth whom one would expect to be a bookworm rather than a hunter. Snyder reported an incredibly large bag, twenty-eight elephants, which set up a record. And Snyder promised I should have part in an elephant hunt, for which I was tremendously eager.

Arrangements went forward for the hunt with speed, so that our anxiety became dulled before the new interest.

Van arrived with the trek wagon, spare parts, fuel and extra provisions. Everyone in Umtali had been friendly and helpful, but there was no lifting of the ban against our traveling through Rhodesia. And trouble was in the air. A report of fire in the bush stirred the whole settlement. We felt rather desperate about the car which had been left behind in the bush. It contained the valuable cameras, equipment, records of our travels all over the world and my precious diary. There were guns and extra ammunition which we had been unable to carry, and trophies and a number of feet of film. Our entire fortune was in it. If we lost film and cameras we were sunk.

The men went back to see if our equipment and records could be salvaged. And then they found that a miracle had happened. As Cap, Van and Owen advanced across the burned-over terrain, they saw the car. We had left it directly on the native trail that led to the water hole from Gomani. The natives daily used that path leading to their only water supply. The car was in the clearing, and the superstitious blacks had gone out of their way around this magic monster which had come roaring out of the south to blockade their accustomed thoroughfare. They had made two new trails, which left the car on an isolated patch of hard sand, with no vegetation near it. The creeping fire, without wind to fan it, died out at the edge of the trails. Our car was absolutely safe; neither man nor elements had hurt our precious cargo of films.

Meg, Smith and I spent practically all our time at the Snyder camp listening to his yarns. He seemed glad to talk to other white people besides Muller. He told how shrewdly cunning elephants are, how dangerous the herds of cows, and the strange solitariness of the bulls. He told of the unbelievable speed of these huge and seemingly clumsy animals. Then Bwana Snyder sent us back to the boma with a side of hippo bacon, which is a delicacy of the Sabi menu.

A few weeks later we commenced our new move toward civilizations. Snyder offered his span of eighteen gray donkeys to transfer our equipment across the river, then to haul over the cars. This last was an historic event, the first time a car crossed the Sabi.

I wanted the motor to be running, so a plan was figured out, and to keep the tradition of my being first on such an enterprise I stood at the wheel of the car as it was dragged across. We had encased the distributor in elephant grease; the carburetor was made into a submarine device by placing an inner tube over it with one end raised far above the water level. The native boys harnessed the donkeys to the traces attached to the front axle. There were loud yells and cracking of *sjamboks*; then as the little gray animals moved, slowly the car slipped from the sandy beach. Water gurgled around the wheels and radiator. I was proud as I heard a low grumble from the motor, and then we had reached the sand bar of the further bank. Cheers rose from both sides of the river as the feat was accomplished, and again as it was repeated with the second car, with Cap at its wheel.

But there was one more thrill before we pushed on to Macequece, and that was the elephant hunt.

For three days we tramped over the veldt. Somehow I acquired the reputation of being a bungler on safari. When I rustled a leaf or tripped over liana, the native boys shook their heads in dismay, and my own gunbearer foretold catastrophic results of having a woman along. He was nearly right.

At daybreak we were on a grassy plain. The game scouts returned with broad grins on their faces; they had sighted elephant. Snyder trained his glasses between distant kopjes and located our objective. We moved forward in silence. Presently Snyder waved us behind a natural barrier of karoo bush at an angle ideal for the wind. In a small green declivity we saw four tuskers raise their trunks at the same moment. They suspected alien presence even before Cap touched the switch of the automatic camera. The strange whir created unease among the elephants, and they flapped their leaflike ears. But I was amazed at their unlikeness to the Indian elephant. I raised my camera to get a still and a bug flew into my eye. Cap kept on, following the animals as they moved.

My eye clear again, I took my gun and Snyder nodded. I took aim and fired. With the report, the rear-guard bull squealed, turned and came toward us. The ground shook beneath his tremendous tread. In that moment my spirit seemed to fly from Africa to Greenland; then Snyder touched my arm, and I cowered behind the bush with my heart thumping.

The elephant stopped, puzzled, fifty yards from our hiding place. Snyder was aiming coolly, but too slowly for me. The elephant spun about, charged again, and again Snyder was ready at the right moment. The big beast fell. Natives rushed up, yellowing with excitement.

"Come and see what they are doing," said Muller, who was along, and he grabbed my arm. I saw that the black boys were cutting the tail off the elephant—taking off the "bush," for good luck.

Snyder had come up and he hustled me away. "They'll gorge on elephant until they're stupid," he said. "This is no place for you."

That day was six weeks from the day of our arrival in Massengena, and four and a half months since our departure from Pafuri. We had to move soon, yet fate was taking another hand in our affairs.

Within Sight of Cairo

AT MASSENGENA I cracked up with malaria. There is nothing very clear in my memory and no entry in my diary between my last glimpse of the tom-tom player at sunset on the Sabi, and a hospital bed where I was told I was in Umtali, which is in the forbidden Rhodesia.

We were to leave Sabi at dawn. Every day at sunrise the giant negro beat reveille and every evening he sounded curfew on the pair of colossal drums, which it took several men to carry to the top of the knoll on the south bank. Each evening I watched this performance in a trance of peculiar fascination; the vibration of the drums seemed to bring a cold chill over everything; crying babies and yapping dogs, chattering women and the shrilly laughing young native girls all silenced before the drum thunder. I wanted a film of the wielding arms in silhouette, and I slipped across the river by myself, taking the camera in its watertight covering.

I forgot about crocodiles, and delayed until the last echoes of those drum beats had gone beyond the horizon. I had to wade the Sabi, and it was after dusk. I jumped into the darkening water and slushed forward against the current. It became too dark to see anything in the river; I was terrified at the gurgle and swirl, which might mean one of the hateful reptiles. I fell, then dragged myself over the sand bar and splashed forward through the more shallow pools. It seemed an eternity before I made the other side and dry land.

There was no way and no time to dry my clothing properly. Meg rose in the night to cook our regular pot of maize to stay us on the first part of the trip. For the first time in months this mealie was fully cooked. I enjoyed every bite, even though we had neither sugar nor milk. It was the only hot meal we could expect in four days.

Long afterward Meg told me the tale of that maize. She had used up the end of a sack of maize and, copying the native women, had cooked it very slowly, stirring constantly. As she stirred, she saw little white maggots appear in increasing number. My sister was Spartan. Dawn was our starting hour and there was no more time for cooking, and no more maize unless she unpacked to open up a fresh supply. Yet that maize porridge was the best I ever tasted.

My next coherent memory is of a hospital bed; there was a nurse, and a doctor who was speaking.

"Far gone," he said, but I found myself hanging on tighter to some invisible support to keep from going further. Something cold seemed to be under my head, and a stab of pain kept coming in my arm, so that I jerked convulsively. They were giving me injections. I found myself floating away, alternately hot and cold, and somewhere in my brain was a recurring nightmarish phrase: "Cap dead—Smith dead—Owen Dead—"

But presently things cleared, and I was quite conscious when a very clean and very sweet-looking nurse directed me to turn my head on the pillow and see who was in the next bed.

"Aloha cherie!"

"Meg!"

I thought I called out, but my voice was only a whisper.

"Both of us with malaria," Meg explained, for she was much stronger than I, since my continued delirium had taken a terrible toll of reserve strength.

"Everybody?" I asked, for the nightmares had been vivid.

"Fine!" said Meg. There was a letter from Cap this morning. He is still in Macequece, had malaria and a touch of black water. He's waiting for us to join him, but he's sending the three boys on here."

"Where is here?" I asked.

"We're in Umtali," Meg explained. It has been Bwana Snyder who had saved us. He had trekked us across the border to hospital, filling us with quinine on the journey, and had helped Meg, ill herself, to restrain me in delirium. It seemed I'd simply collapsed and Cap had sent a runner back to Snyder for aid.

It was several days after my return to consciousness that Van, Owen and Smith, walking on tiptoe and nervously twirling their terrais, visited me, carrying offerings of tight bunches of English garden flowers, culled from the garden of the kindly Umtali householder where they had lodging. The boys were embarrassed, but full of sincere feeling. Smith told me I looked wonderful after my illness.

"I myself personally think so too," mocked Owen at Smith's speech, and he promptly retaliated with the Cockney's idea of American: "I guess, reckon and calculate just that."

Smith was nervous, for this was his farewell. He was making an easy trip south, and Van, too, was leaving us, returning to his home, where he had joined our outfit. I said goodbye sorrowfully for the boys had been good sports and excellent travelling companions.

"We have a capital of twenty-two pounds," said Owen suddenly, after the other two men had gone. "The Portuguese authorities are holding Cap for a twenty-pound sterling deposit per person if we return to their territory; the Rhodesian travel ban is still on. If they'd only give in, the way via Salisbury and Victoria Falls would be a snap after what we have come through."

But the authorities at Salisbury would not give in; and Portuguese East, satisfied at last that we had no money for deposits, gave us transit rather than have us die of starvation encamped at their border.

Slowly, but with infinitely greater ease, we were on the road again, crossing Tanganyika; and weeks later we went into Kenya Colony, steadily moving north. It seemed now that officialdom could not do enough for us; they made our way easy, and our welcomes at bomas by the District commissioner.

When it came time for us to cross the Athi plains we had excited warnings that we should not drive out from the settlement. A man and his wife had driven some distance out on the road we had to follow; they had been attacked by rhinoceros. These are fierce animals, and stupid too. Rhino will charge a large boulder when enraged as readily as they will an automobile, as they had done in this case. Both passengers were torn to shreds, and their open touring car left a heap of scrap, as discovered by the rescue party which left when runners brought in the alarm. As usual, officials thought us completely crazed, and perhaps our party, now consisting of Meg, myself, Cap and Owen, was little distraught. Owen began to show signs of malaria, Cap's hands and mine shook as we held the steering wheel of our respective cars, and Meg was on the verge of a relapse. I knew I was close to another collapse. But it seemed impossible to give up.

We were the first travelers out from Nairobi on the rhino-infested highroad. It was not bad travel as to surface, but Cap's car burned out a bearing as we reached the very place of the recent tragedy. We took turns standing on the hood of the second car to scan the terrain through glasses, while Owen repaired the damage. We saw moving masses of ugly flesh among patches of scrub and mud pans, but no rhino sighted us; their insensate fury of some days before must have died down.

As we got into the regular routine of travel we began to feel better, and we had an unforgettable week at Lake Victoria Nyanza, circled first by Stanley and discovered by

Speke. It lies half in the British Protectorate of Uganda, and half in what was German East Africa. We were awestruck at its size, estimated at twenty-six thousand square miles. On its banks we came to a kraal of the extraordinary Kavirondo.

This was a nervous, thrilling and spine-chilling week such as may be chanced on only once in a lifetime by white travelers. The Kavirondo were having a funeral celebration. There was a wailing chorus of two thousand voices echoing across the veldt. The white Commissioner warned us the natives were drunk with trade gin and quantities of potent Kaffir beer, a powerful liquid. They were staging stupendous attacks again the evil spirits which follow the dead. We caught glimpses of the blacks bedecked in masses of ostrich-feather finery.

Then came Uganda proper and the Southern Sudan, and we assured ourselves Cairo was within sight. We drank in the luxuriant beauty of a smiling Africa, and counted only fifteen hundred more miles of swamp and desert land between us and the oriental city where I had joined the expedition more than four years before.

The District Commissioner at Mongalla dealt us the first blow, although with reluctance: "You will have to abandon the route via the French Congo and Lake Chad, and across the edge of the Sahara," he said. "Unprecedented rains have inundated the Lake Chad section and it will not be passable for months."

That forced the itinerary to change to north from Mongalla by the swamps of Bahr el Arab and from there to Khartoum. As we reorganized equipment and sought for additions to our personnel, the torrential rains swept eastward to Mongalla. I felt pretty hopeless, and I knew our cause was lost when Cap came in from a conference with the Commissioner at the boma.

"There's a Dinka uprising," he said.

That was the end. I was not to complete the Cape-to-Cairo drive—not this time.

The Dinkas are changeable in mood as Africa herself, sometimes smiling with good will and at other times snarling with hostility. These Dinkas are a huge people, created with an incredible ugliness of feature. They sleep in the ashes of their own fires, and smear their cattle, too, with wood ashes to free them of the insects that swarm in the swamps among which the Dinka homes are made. A Dinka uprising means fear and horror to the small outposts of the Upper Sudan. Now they had murdered a District Commissioner, and were on a mad spree of burning villages, driving off cattle, pillaging, robbing and slaughtering among their hereditary and sworn enemies, the Arabs.

Owen went down completely with a bad bout of malaria. All of our bodies were demanding rest, and our funds were distressingly low.

"There's one way out," said Cap. "We can return to Mombasa on the east coast, and from there take a ship to Alexandria.

The German East African Line at Mombasa favored my cabled proposal, and gave us choice of two sailings, one leaving in ten days and another in five weeks' time.

Owen staggered up from his sick bed. "I can make it," he said. I wondered if he could or if any of us could, but to stay five weeks more in the same place was financially impossible.

The rains commenced on the day we left to dash to Mombasa. Black clouds sailed up from the west, there was the noise of distant thunder, and a dry gale swept everything before it. Banana plants lay low; trees, thornbush and everything else was flattened. Owen and Cap were not in camp when this wind came. Meg and I cowered under a tarpaulin; then after the wind storm subsided the water descended from the heavens in sheets, until the hillside on which we had our camp was marked by gushing rivulets. When the rain stopped, the temperature had dropped so that we shook with the sudden cold.

"November fifteenth is sailing date," said Cap, who now peered round the tarpaulin edge, "and we've simply got to make it."

Mongalla disappeared behind us, then came Rhino camp; three ferry crossings, and Jinja and Kismu were reached and passed. This forced travel through fierce rain, with trails like troughs of mud, seemed beyond human power. We did not think—we seemed numb to feeling; we just kept going under the momentum of need.

We lost our way en route to Nakuru, the second mistake we had made in two days, for landmarks seemed washed from existence on what ordinarily is a simple track to follow. Meg and I waited while Cap and Owen drove back to the last road fork to find out our error. Meg held a candle for me under the tarpaulin, and I brought my diary up to date; then my pencil jumped and made a quavering line, for a leopard howled. As the sound died away I wrote: "It seems like the scream of a woman in sickening agony, as the sound cuts across the plain with terrible regularity."

It was four hours later when Cap and Owen returned. "We are on the right road after all," they said.

I started my car, and in twenty minutes the lights of Nakuru were blinking through the gloom of the downpour. Four hours of our precious time had been wasted while we were lost merely in our minds.

There were forty-eight hours more of driving, and a thirty-minute half at Nairobi. A letter from my mother had lain there for us, and in it she announced her imminent return to the States from Jamaica. We picked up a heartening cable from Mombasa at the Nairobi railroad station, then pushed on. I still wondered if we could make that ship. Meg's eyes had the sparkle of fever and there was an unhealthy flush on her wan cheeks; Owen as I studied him was a pitiful object. All his bronze-red glow of health was gone, and he looked a thoroughly sick man. Cap, I could not deny it, was distressing to see, with sunken eyes glittering, and his once sun-tan complexion now a sallow clay. I could not see myself, for somewhere a native woman had purloined the mirror, but I could guess at my appearance from my feelings.

A mist rose over rain-drenched earth as we crossed the Athi plains beyond Nairobi, and near Kilimanjaro came one of those last straws which cause despair. The frame of my car broke close to the side motor bracket, the engine sagged and the driveshaft was slightly twisted. There was terrific labor as Cap and Owen inserted a wooden splint in the frame and lashed it with rope and lengths of wire. It held the motor off the ground, but how long it would keep turning was only a guess. Yet this overcoming of a bad mishap seemed to have given everyone a second wind. I actually felt the old exhilaration of combat steal over me, that do-or-die, conquer-every-obstacle idea which flavored our early months on the road. All four of us confessed to this queer renewal of spirit after we got aboard ship, and Cap and I told Meg and Owen unending stories of Arabia, India, China and Japan and the mad rushing months in the United States. I believe now the great truth of our internal excitement was the thought of home.

I think at the end of the hundred and ninety-two hours of that mad race to the coast, we were all crazed with fever. But at midnight on November 14, we were to find ourselves twenty miles from the pontoon crossing at Mombasa. It was quite clearly stated on the first civilized signpost we had seen since we left Capetown. The road improved, imperceptibly at first, but as the miles passed under our lagging wheels, very definitely. If the cars would just hold together! A dripping forest ended abruptly and before us we saw the Indian Ocean, or at least a small portion of it. We spread the largest tarpaulin on the sodden clay by the pontoon landing and were asleep even as we threw ourselves prone.

Scorching rays of sun awoke me. My face felt seared, and steam rose from my clothing and that of the others as they still slept; mist rose, too, from the jungle tract behind us, making a hothouse odor of decaying vegetation.

Though tired to death, I could not remain still, so I went down the slipway to the wooden landing, and looked across the strait to Mombasa. Three miles up that jungle-bordered channel is the Kilindini steamer anchorage. I could see no outline that might suggest a battle-gray German freighter. But I saw a Goanese lounging two hundred yards away. I approached him and spoke to him in English, which he understood.

"Has the German liner sailed?"

The man saluted. "I am not certain, Memsahib, but I believe a gray boat sailed at daybreak."

With conceit over former triumphs and anticipated success, we had set foot on South African soil, and I fear I had a certain amount of bumptiousness in my desire to show the residents that what they said could not be done, could be accomplished—maybe not by them, but most certainly by us. But it seemed that Africa was a feline, graceful and treacherous, and now I wondered if she were about to play a last practical joke on us who had, with so much youthful arrogance, thought to conquer her. At least we had done the greatest part of all that we had set out to accomplish.

I rejoined the others and we crossed to Mombasa. I did not dare repeat the doubt the casual East Indian had put into my mind. But he was right: a gray painted vessel had sailed on the dawn tide turn. Thank heaven, it was not our ship.

The vessel for Port Said was exactly twenty-four hours late. Had it not been—oh, well, there's no use speculating, but life seems shot with coincidences.

"I'll come back to Africa," I said to Cap as we stood by the rail and watched Owen superintending the lashing of the two battered cars on the after deck.

"I've a better idea," said I. I looked at Cap a bit apprehensively, even though he was looking much more like his former self, for the enforced stopover in Mombasa had yielded shaves and haircuts for the men, while for Meg and me it had meant baths and the luxury of a pot of face cream and a package of powder.

"What's your idea, Aloha?" Cap spoke more or less idly, so that my next words caught him off guard.

"Well, why the same continent twice? If you're willing, and after our lecture tour is finished in the States, I was thinking of South America—Amazon head hunters and Inca cities—oh, you know, all that below the equator, practically on the other side of the world."

Cap strolled aft to speak with the skipper. I threw up my head and sniffed in the salt hot tang of the Indian Ocean.

"What are you shouting about?" asked Meg, who came alongside me.

"Oh, nothing: I just said...South America!"

ALOHA WANDERWELL FILM FRAMES

The Wanderwell expedition was partially financed by personal appearances and vaudeville-styled presentations in which Aloha would show films of their travels and tell stories of their adventures on the road. After the Wanderwells returned to the United States, Aloha herself edited together the highlights into a feature length documentary that was released in 1929 under the title, "Car and Camera Round The World." Many of her original films still survive, and efforts are now underway to properly preserve and restore the delicate and extremely flammable nitrate film. The following images all derive from master film elements held by the Nile Baker Estate.

Japan, 1924

Aloha en route to Hawaii, 1924

Aloha with Mary Pickford in Hollywood, 1925

China, 1924

Africa, 1927.

Siberia, 1924

Hawaii, 1925

At home in Newport Beach, California, 1949

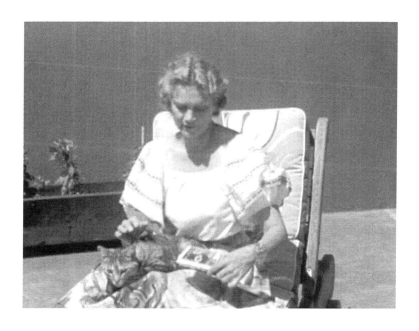

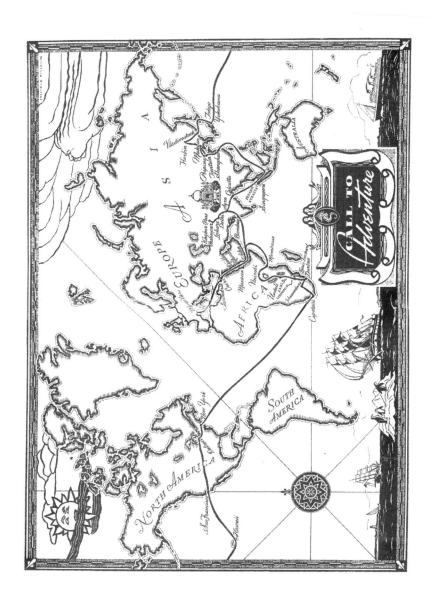

279